Our Internet Society

ISSUES

Volume 104

20 M.

3 n

1

Editor

Craig Donnellan

Independence

Educational Publishers
Cambridge

Stevenson College Edinburgh
Bankhead Ave EDIN EH11 4DE

First published by Independence
PO Box 295
Cambridge CB1 3XP
England

British Library Cataloguing in Publication Data
Our Internet Society – (Issues Series)
I. Donnellan, Craig II. Series
303.4'833

ISBN 1 86168 324 3

Printed in Great Britain
MWL Print Group Ltd

Typeset by
Lisa Firth

Cover
The illustration on the front cover is by
Don Hatcher.

CONTENTS

Chapter One: Our Internet Society

Chapter Two: Dangers of the Internet

Introduction

Our Internet Society is the one hundred and fourth volume in the **Issues** series. The aim of this series is to offer up-to-date information about important issues in our world.

Our Internet Society looks at the role of the Internet in today's society and the dangers posed by the Internet.

The information comes from a wide variety of sources and includes:
Government reports and statistics
Newspaper reports and features
Magazine articles and surveys
Website material
Literature from lobby groups
and charitable organisations.

It is hoped that, as you read about the many aspects of the issues explored in this book, you will critically evaluate the information presented. It is important that you decide whether you are being presented with facts or opinions. Does the writer give a biased or an unbiased report? If an opinion is being expressed, do you agree with the writer?

Our Internet Society offers a useful starting-point for those who need convenient access to information about the many issues involved. However, it is only a starting-point. At the back of the book is a list of organisations which you may want to contact for further information.

*****

An introduction to the Internet

Information from SOFWeb

What is the Internet?

The Internet is made up of millions of computers linked together around the world in such a way that information can be sent from any computer to any other 24 hours a day. These computers can be in homes, schools, universities, government departments, or businesses small and large. They can be any type of computer and be single personal computers or workstations on a school or a company network.

> *The Internet is made up of millions of computers linked together around the world in such a way that information can be sent from any computer to any other 24 hours a day*

The Internet is often described as 'a network of networks' because all the smaller networks of organisations are linked together into the one giant network called the Internet. All computers are pretty much equal once connected to the Internet, the only difference will be the speed of the connection which is dependent on your Internet Service Provider and your own modem.

The Internet has developed a very strong community base where information, software and expert advice are freely shared and for this reason users have developed a very strong protective stance on freedom of speech, freedom from commercial interests, netiquette and unsuitable material on the web.

Why would you want to use it?

There are so many things you can do and participate in once connected to the Internet. They include using a range of services to communicate and share information and things quickly and inexpensively with tens of millions of people, both young and old and from diverse cultures around the world. For example:

■ You'll be able to keep in touch and send things to colleagues and friends using electronic mail, Internet telephone, keyboard chat and video conferencing.

■ You can also tap into thousands of databases, libraries and newsgroups around the world to gather information on any topics of interest for work or recreation. The information can be in the form of text, pictures or even video material.

■ This means you can stay up to date with news, sports, weather and any current affairs around the world with information updated daily, hourly or instantly.

■ You can also locate and download computer software and other products that are available in cyberspace.

■ You can listen to sounds and music, and watch digital movies.

■ There are also a growing number of interactive multimedia games and educational tools.

And as well as using the Internet for receiving things you will be able to publish information about your school, hobbies or interests.

A brief history of cyberspace

Although it may seem like a new idea, the net has actually been around for over 40 years. It all began in the US during the Cold War, as a university experiment in military communications. By linking lots of computers together in a network,

rather than serially (in a straight line), the Pentagon thought that in the event of a nuclear attack on the US it was unlikely that the entire network would be damaged, and therefore they would still be able to send and receive intelligence.

At first each computer was physically linked by cable to the next computer, but this approach has obvious limitations, which led to the development of networks utilising the telephone system. Predictably, people found that nuclear strike or not, they could talk to each other using this computer network, and some university students started using this network to do their homework together.

It seems a natural human characteristic to want to communicate, and once people realised that they could talk to other people via this computer network they began to demand access, although initially the users were only from the university and government sectors. But more and more people could see the potential of computer networks, and various community groups developed networks separate from the official networks for the use of their local communities.

The sum of all these various local, regional and national networks is the Internet as we experience it today, an ever-expanding network of people, computers and information coming together in ways the Pentagon never dreamed of 40 years ago. So what began as an exercise in military paranoia has become a method of global communication.

'Cyberspace' is a term coined by William Gibson in his fantasy novel *Neuromancer* to describe the 'world' of computers, and the society that gathers around them. Gibson's fantasy of a world of connected computers has moved into a present reality in the form of the Internet. In cyberspace people 'exist' in the ether – you meet them electronically, in a disembodied, faceless form.

The Internet and the World Wide Web

Sometimes people use the words Internet and World Wide Web (WWW) synonymously but they are different. The WWW is a component of the Internet that presents information in a graphical interface. You can think of the WWW as the illustrated version of the Internet. It began in the late 1980s when physicist Dr Berners-Lee wrote a small computer program for his own personal use. This program allowed pages, within his computer, to be linked together using keywords. It soon became possible to link documents in different computers, as long as they were connected to the Internet. The document formatting language used to link documents is called HTML (Hypertext Markup Language).

The Web remained primarily text based until 1992. Two events occurred that year that forever changed the way the Web looked. Marc Andreesen developed a new computer program called the NCSA Mosaic and gave it away! The NCSA Mosaic was the first Web browser.

The browser made it easier to access the different Web sites that had started to appear. Soon Web sites contained more than just text, they also had sound and video files. The development of the WWW has been the catalyst for the popularity of the Internet and is also the easiest part of the Internet to use. We now have Internet Chat, Discussion Groups, Internet Phone capabilities, Video conferencing, News Groups, Interactive Multimedia, Games and so much more.

TCP/IP

TCP/IP is a communications protocol used to transfer digital data around the Internet. TCP and IP were developed by a Department of Defense (DOD) research project to connect different networks designed by different vendors into a network of networks (the 'Internet'). TCP/IP is often referred to as the 'Internet protocol'.

As with all communications protocols, TCP/IP is composed of layers:

IP – is responsible for moving packets of data from node to node. IP forwards each packet based on a four byte destination address (the IP number). The Internet authorities assign ranges of numbers to different organisations. The organisations assign groups of their numbers to departments. IP operates on gateway machines that move data from department to organisation to region and then around the world.

TCP – is responsible for verifying the correct delivery of data from client to server. Data can be lost in the intermediate network. TCP adds support to detect errors or lost data and to trigger retransmission until the data is correctly and completely received.

Sockets – is a name given to the package of subroutines that provide access to TCP/IP on most systems.

■ The above information is reprinted with kind permission from SOFWeb – for more information please visit their web page at www.sofweb.vic.edu.au

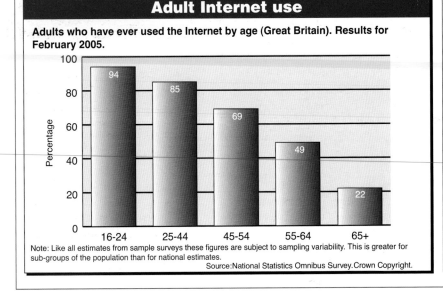

Adult Internet use

Adults who have ever used the Internet by age (Great Britain). Results for February 2005.

Note: Like all estimates from sample surveys these figures are subject to sampling variability. This is greater for sub-groups of the population than for national estimates.

Source: National Statistics Omnibus Survey. Crown Copyright.

UK children go online

Surveying the experiences of young people and their parents

Key findings on access and inequalities

Internet access and use is widespread among UK children and young people, being considerably higher than among adults and among the highest in Europe. However, significant inequalities persist especially in home access. Continuing changes in the nature and quality of access indicate fast-rising standards and expectations.

Homes with children lead in gaining Internet access: they are also now acquiring multiple computers plus broadband access to the Internet

---

Among all 9 to 19-year-olds:

- Home access is growing: Three-quarters (75%) have accessed the Internet from a computer at home. Currently, 74% have Internet access via a computer, games console or digital television while one quarter of 9 to 19-year-olds (23%) have never accessed the Internet on a computer from home, and 29% currently lack such access.
- School access is near universal: 92% have accessed the Internet at school, and one-quarter (24%) have access at school but not at home. However, two-thirds (64%) have also used the Internet elsewhere.
- Socio-economic differences are sizeable: 88% of middle-class but only 61% of working-class children have accessed the Internet at home; 86% of children in areas of low deprivation in England have used the Internet on a computer at home compared with 66% in areas of high deprivation.

- Homes with children lead in gaining Internet access: They are also now acquiring multiple computers plus broadband access to the Internet – 36% have more than one computer at home, and 24% live in a household with broadband access.
- Access platforms are diversifying: 87% have a computer at home (71% with Internet access), 62% have digital television (17% with Internet access), 82% have a games console (8% with Internet access), and 81% have their own mobile phone (38% with Internet access).
- Many computers in private rooms: One-fifth (19%) have Internet access in their bedroom – 22% of boys versus 15% of girls, 21% middle class versus 16% working class, 10% of 9 to 11-year-olds versus 26% of 16 to 17-year-olds. Fewer than half the computers online at home are located in a public room, and four-fifths (79%) of those with home access report mostly using the Internet alone.

Key findings on the nature of Internet use

Most young people use the Internet frequently though often for moderate amounts of time. They use the Internet for a wide range of purposes, not all of which are socially approved.

- Most are daily or weekly users: 9 to 19-year-olds are mainly divided between daily users (41%) and weekly users (43%). Only 13% are occasional users, and just 3% count as non-users.
- Most online for less than an hour: One-fifth (19%) of 9 to 19-year-olds spend about ten minutes per day online, half spend between about half an hour (25%) and one hour (23%) online, and a further fifth go online for between one (14%) and three hours (6%) each day. One in 20 (5%) spend more than three hours online on an average day.

- More time spent watching TV or with the family: Time spent online is still less than time spent watching television or with the family, but it is similar to that spent doing homework and playing computer games and greater than time spent on the phone or reading.
- Most use it for searching and homework: Among the 84% of 9 to 19-year-olds who use the Internet daily or weekly, 90% use it to do work for school or college, 94% use it to get information for other things, 72% use it to send and receive emails, 70% to play games online, 55% to send and receive instant messages, 45% to download music and 21% to use chat rooms. Further, 44% look for information on careers and further education, 40% look for products or shop online, and 26% read the news.

- Some use it for less-approved activities: Among 12 to 19-year-olds who go online daily or weekly, 21% admit to having copied something from the Internet for a school project and handed it in as their own, 8% claim to have hacked into someone else's website or email, 5% have visited an online dating site, and 4% have sent a message to make someone feel uncomfortable or threatened.

One in six (16%) 9 to 19-year-olds make low levels or even no use of the Internet, and even among more frequent users, use is often narrow.

- Non-use not just a matter of lack of interest: Access and expertise remain significant issues – 47% of occasional and non-users say that they lack access, 25% are not interested, 15% say they don't know how to use the Internet, and 14% lack the time to use it.
- Even frequent users make narrow use of the web: Among those who go online at least once a week, half concentrate their use on fewer than five different websites.

Key findings on education, learning and literacy

- Many have not received lessons on how to use the Internet: Despite the stress laid on ICT in education policy, nearly one-third (30%) of pupils report having received no lessons at all on using the Internet, although most have been taught something – 23% report having received 'a lot' of lessons, 28% 'some' and 19% 'just one or two'.
- Skills gap between parents and children: Children usually consider themselves more expert than their parents – 28% of parents who use the Internet describe themselves as beginners compared with only 7% of children who go online daily or weekly, and only 12% of parents consider themselves advanced compared with 32% of children. While most parents and children are confident in their searching skills, among parents only 1 in 3 know how to set up an email account, and only a fifth or fewer are able to set up a filter, remove a virus, download music or fix a problem.
- Children lack key skills in evaluating online content: Four in ten pupils aged 9 to 19 trust most of the information on the Internet, half trust some of it, and only 1 in 10 are sceptical about much information online. Only 33% of 9 to 19-year-olds who go online at least once a week say that they have been told how to judge the reliability

---

Children lack key skills in evaluating online content: Four in ten pupils aged 9-19 trust most of the information on the Internet

---

of online information, and among parents of 9 to 17-year-olds, only 41% are confident that their child has learned how to judge the reliability of online information.

Thus, there is considerable scope for increasing the Internet-related skills and literacy of both children and their parents. Many children are using the Internet without skills in critical evaluation, and many parents lack the skills to guide and support their children's Internet use.

Key findings on pornography online

Coming into contact with pornography is, the UKCGO survey shows, a commonplace but often unwelcome experience for children and young people.

Among 9 to 19-year-olds who go online at least once a week:

- More than half have seen pornography online: Nearly six in ten (57%) have come into contact with online pornography. However, only 16% of parents think that their child has seen pornography on the Internet.
- Most porn is viewed unintentionally: 38% have seen a pornographic pop-up advert while doing something else, 36% have accidentally found themselves on a pornographic website when looking for something else, 25% have received pornographic junk mail by email or instant messaging, 10% have visited a pornographic website on purpose, 9% have been sent pornography from someone they know, and 2% have been sent pornography from someone they met online.
- More porn on the Internet than in other media: Among teens (12-19 years), 68% claim to have seen pornography on the Internet, 20% saying 'many times'. Moreover, 53% of parents consider

(and children agree) that the Internet is more likely to expose children to pornography than are television, video or magazines.

- Mixed responses to online porn: When young people encounter pornography on the Internet, half claim not to be bothered by it, but a significant minority do not like it, and one-quarter of 9 to 15-year-olds who have seen porn say they were disgusted. Half of those who encounter online pornography leave the site as quickly as they can, while the others say they look at it, tell a friend or parent, click on the links or return to it later.
- Too young to have seen it: Interestingly, nearly half (45%) of 18 to 19-year-old Internet users who have seen any pornography (online or offline) now think they were too young to see it when they first did.

Key findings on communication and participation

Rather than seeing face-to-face communication as automatically superior, young people evaluate the different forms of communication available to them according to distinct communicative needs. The mobile phone is fast overtaking the desktop computer as a prioritised means of communication.

Among 9 to 19-year-olds who use the Internet at least once a week:

- The mobile phone is the preferred method of communication: Whether for passing time, making arrangements, getting advice, gossiping or flirting, the phone and text messaging are preferred over emailing or instant messaging (IM).
- Most online communication is with local friends: Contact with people that children have not met face to face, on the other hand, occurs mainly among the 21% who visit chat rooms.
- Talking online is less satisfying but has its advantages: A third (33%) of email, IM and chat users think that talking to people on the Internet is at least as satisfying as talking to them in real life, and a quarter of children and young people identify significant advantages to online communication in terms of privacy, confidence and intimacy. Further, a

quarter of 12 to 19-year-olds who use the Internet at least weekly say they go online to get advice.

- Not all use is receptive but, rather, interactive: 44% have completed a quiz online, 25% have sent an email or text message to a website, 22% have voted for something online, 17% have sent pictures or stories to a website, 17% have contributed to a message board, and 8% have filled in a form. Most active of all, 34% have set up their own website. Further, 9% have offered advice to others while 8% have signed a petition.
- Some are interested in civic issues: 55% of 12 to 19-year-olds who use the Internet at least weekly have sought out sites concerned with political or civic issues, although two-fifths are not interested. However, only a minority have responded to or contributed to these sites in any way.

- The above information is from the Executive Summary of UK Children Go Online, published by the UK Children Go Online project. For more information visit their website which can be found at www.children-go-online.net

© London School of Economics

E-shopping continues to surge

Information from the British Market Research Bureau (BMRB)

By Paul Milsom

The number of e-shoppers has reached its highest level yet and now stands at 16 million – around 1.3 million higher than May 2004.

This new peak, as measured by the Internet Monitor, also probably reflects a renewed faith in the Internet as a tool for conducting shopping – particularly for summer items such as holidays.

The average online spend amongst e-shoppers (in the last six months) has increased to £605 from £572 in May 2004. Total annual Internet spend is now put at £19.4 billion – a ten per cent increase on August last year.

Among users of the Internet who have not yet bought online, concern over credit card security is still the most cited reason, mentioned by 27

per cent. This is down from 31 per cent in May, reflecting a general improvement in confidence in the security of E-commerce. This improvement in confidence has been the long-term trend but there was a dip in confidence earlier this year.

Almost a fifth (18 per cent) of Internet users who have yet to buy online say they still prefer the personal contact of going into a shop.

eBay maintains its position as the most visited e-commerce site in the last four weeks (5 September-5 October 2004) at 51 per cent of the online population, an increase of five percentage points since May. Amazon.co.uk has moved back up to number two with 37 per cent.

Argos has also slightly improved its percentage of visitors in the last four weeks but has slipped back to third overall due to Amazon's gains.

eBay also continues to enjoy the highest awareness of all the e-commerce sites measured (91 per cent – up from 78 per cent just one year ago).

Meanwhile, Tesco remains the most-visited supermarket site, visited by 23 per cent of Internet users in the last four weeks, followed by Sainsbury's (12 per cent), Asda (nine per cent), Iceland (six per cent), Safeway (five per cent), and Ocado (two per cent).

- Information from the BMRB – see page 41 for address details or visit www.bmrb.co.uk

© British Market Research Bureau (BMRB)

Internet shopping

Best practices – information from CyberAngels

Some of the best practices are the same for physical shopping as well as shopping on the net:

- Use common sense to avoid offers too good to be true
- Check the warranty and return policy of the merchant
- Check the reputation of the merchant before shopping
- Use a secure browser
- Keep a record
- Read the privacy policy before submitting information

Safe shopping online

1. If you have many credit cards, use only one card for online transactions for easy tracking.
2. Use credit cards in preference to debit card/checking account since you are protected totally against fraud losses in excess of $50 in case of credit card.
3. Store details of all online purchases and check against your monthly statement. Report your card issuer immediately if any unauthorised charges are found in your statement.
4. Review the online merchant rating (from services like TRUSTe,

BBBOnline or WebTrust). Companies with brick and mortar counterpart are generally more safe than net only merchants.

5. System security:
- Enable alerts in your browser when you are diverted from a secure server to non-secure server.
- Do not store password/ personal details in your computer.
- Change your password frequently. Create passwords as combination of special characters, numerals and letters. Do not use words in dictionary or personal details as part of password since these are easier to crack.
- Do not access mails containing username/password for the services subscribed from public Internet sources like school/ Library/Cybercafe. The next user may be able to access these details from history/temp files.
- Enable intrusion alert program for your computer. Frequently delete unwanted cookies from your system.

6. Your card details are relatively safe with merchant having secure payment processing. Signs like a symbol of lock on the browser bar and the site address starting like 'https://' indicates that you are connected to a secure server and your card data is encrypted by SSL (secure socket layer). This ensures that your card data is encrypted while reaching the merchant.

7. Do not send payment information/personal information/card details via non-secure email. They may be intercepted by packet sniffers.

- The above information is from CyberAngels – see page 41 for contact details or visit their website at www.cyberangels.org

© *CyberAngels*

They flash their cash with a click

As online shopping grows, a new group of consumers is emerging. They have plenty of money and the confidence to buy both big-ticket and run-of-the-mill items online

By Caroline Parry

About 4.2 million people now spend £600 or more online every six months. Exploring the demographic make-up, lifestyle, media habits and attitudes of this lucrative group can pay dividends when brands are looking at ways of influencing them.

New research from BMRB International shows that these high-spenders are concentrated in London and East Anglia. Indeed, Internet users in the London ITV region are 23 per cent more likely to be high online spenders than Internet users as a whole, whilst those in the East of England ITV region are 26 per cent more likely to be. Three-fifths of the online high-spending group are men.

The group's age-profile is skewed towards 35- to 54-year-olds, and particularly towards the high end of this age range: 30 per cent of high-spenders are between 45 and 54 years old, compared with 23 per cent aged between 35 and 44 years old. This older bias is reflected in the level of household income – 45- to 54-year-old high-spenders are 51 per cent more likely than Internet users as a whole to have a pre-tax household income of £50,000 or more.

The more extravagant online spenders are more likely to buy high-value individual products than are the great mass of online shoppers (defined as anyone who has bought online in the past six months). Categories such as property, cars, holidays, computers, other electrical goods and furniture all appear in the top ten types of item bought by the high-spenders.

However, the top-ten list also includes lower-value items that are bought more frequently. High online spenders are 173 per cent more likely than online shoppers as a whole to have bought alcohol, music, flowers and food over the Internet.

The relative enthusiasm of high online spenders for making online

The guide to online grocery shoppers

- 1.7 million people, 4% of GB adults, have bought groceries through the web in the past 6 months.

- Two-thirds of online grocery shoppers are female. They are 37% more likely to be aged between 35 and 44 compared to Internet users as a whole.

- Members of this group are 78% more likely to regularly read the *Financial Times* and 23% more likely to regularly read the *Daily Mail* and the *Metro* than all Internet users.

- When asked what the most important factor is in choosing where to shop, online grocery shoppers are 55% more likely than all Internet users to mention 'loyalty schemes'.

- They are 35% more likely to use pop up blocking software than Internet users as a whole and 53% more likely to strongly agree with the statement 'I like to receive emails from companies'.

- Online grocery shoppers are over 4 times more likely to purchase beer, wine and spirits online and over 3 times more likely to purchase furniture online. However, they are less likely than other Internet users to purchase sports equipment or financial products online.

- They are over twice as likely to cite QVC and Eurosport as their favourite TV channels than Internet users as a whole.

- Online grocery shoppers are over twice as likely to visit bol.com and 88% more likely to visit Zoom than other Internet users. They are also more likely than other Internet users to visit Debenhams and Dominos Pizza websites.

- The above information is from the British Market Research Bureau – for more information visit www.bmrb.co.uk, or see page 41 for address details.

© BMRB

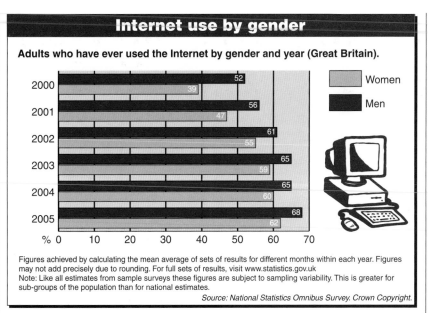

Internet use by gender

Adults who have ever used the Internet by gender and year (Great Britain).

	Women	Men
2000	39	52
2001	47	56
2002	55	61
2003	59	65
2004	60	65
2005	62	68

Figures achieved by calculating the mean average of sets of results for different months within each year. Figures may not add precisely due to rounding. For full sets of results, visit www.statistics.gov.uk

Note: Like all estimates from sample surveys these figures are subject to sampling variability. This is greater for sub-groups of the population than for national estimates.

Source: National Statistics Omnibus Survey. Crown Copyright.

purchases means there are few products they do not buy over the Internet. Having said this, they are ten per cent less likely to have bought CDs, 26 per cent less likely to have bought tickets for events and 50 per cent less likely to have gambled online than are Internet users as a whole. This reflects the demographic profile of the high- spending group.

The high-spending group's propensity for buying big-ticket individual items is reflected in the value of their most recent purchase. High online spenders are almost three-and-a-half times as likely as online shoppers generally to have spent £400 or more on their most recent Web purchase.

One of the key factors that motivates high-spenders to buy online is saving time. This group is 34 per cent more likely than online shoppers generally to agree that they do have time to go to high street shops or shopping centres. However, they also enjoy the time they spend online and are 22 per cent more likely to enjoy shopping online more than on the high street.

The BMRB data shows that almost three-quarters (73 per cent) of high online spenders say that they have been prompted to make an online purchase in the past month by some form of advertising. This compares with 68 per cent of all online shoppers.

Indeed, the higher spenders are 30 per cent more likely than online shoppers as a whole to say they have

been influenced to make a purchase by promotional email or an ad seen in a computing magazine. They are over 20 per cent more likely to have been influenced by ads in Sunday newspapers and through Teletext, Web-based advertising and poster advertising.

High-spenders are 31 per cent more likely than the average Internet user to have a broadband Internet connection. Their heavy Web usage means they visit many sites more frequently than Internet users as a whole. Most notably, they are approximately twice as likely to have

visited Ananova, UK plus, This Is London and FT.com in the past four weeks.

Members of this group still spend more time watching television than consuming any other medium, but they do not watch as much as other types of consumer. They are most likely to watch programmes about sport, current affairs, property or holidays.

Online high-spenders tend to be avid readers of broadsheets compared with all Internet users. They are 54 per cent more likely to read the *Financial Times* and 34 per cent more likely to read *The Guardian*. On Sundays, they are 66 per cent more likely to read *The Independent on Sunday* and 39 per cent more likely to read *The Observer*.

The Internet's big spenders are a time-poor, cash-rich group – a highly attractive target for any e-tailer. This group is amenable to persuasion by advertising, so it is well worth marketers' while to understand their media and lifestyle choices, the better to communicate with them effectively.

■ The above information is from the British Market Research Bureau– for more visit www.bmrb.co.uk, or see page 41 for address details.

© BMRB

Transforming learning and children's services

The e-strategy

Why we need a focus on technology

Achieving our ambitions

Technology has been used in education for many years. It has not yet transformed teaching and learning, but it has made a major impact in many schools, colleges and universities. It has also made information more accessible and administration more efficient.

But ICT can have a greater impact on our wider ambitions for education and children's services. We want children, learners and parents to have more say in those services and we want courses and services to become more personalised. Information and communication technologies (ICT) make this possible provided that we have both the imagination and the right strategic planning. We need to focus both on e-learning – using ICT to change how we learn, and e-delivery – the mechanisms by which we provide electronic information and services.

Why do we need e-learning?

At any stage of learning, ICT could re-engage the unmotivated learner, and bring an authentic and challenging task within their grasp. Or ICT could make the difference between the boredom of the learner who's always left behind, and the discovery that they can find their own way to make progress.

For teachers it can be the difference between learners who are unmotivated, and a class that wants to participate. But it need not involve more time. Head teachers and leaders can work more efficiently and support their teachers better. Teachers given the means to experiment discover their own ways of using their time better.

We do not argue for a complete switch to new technology. Traditional pedagogy and e-learning can and should complement each other. The new technologies are capable of creating real energy and excitement for all age groups. Used well, they should motivate, personalise, and stretch.

Why do we need e-delivery?

Communications technologies are often more readily accessible ways to deliver information and advice than print. Some of the most powerful testimony to the value of ICT comes from people in the most vulnerable groups in our society, who value the social equality, the contact and privacy that ICT offers.

Online information systems, advice and guidance can change how every citizen engages with public services. Of course, many people prefer to meet public servants face to face, but their encounter can be more productive when both sides are better prepared – online services can help that process. This is why we emphasise the importance of joining up agencies to deliver online information and services. We all want to find the information and advice we need quickly. We want to have the opportunity to register or enrol for courses without having to travel or queue. It is important that accessing such services is straightforward and easy for everybody.

What will ICT do for teachers?

For technology to work well, we need good teachers and tutors making good use of it. This is as true of the interactive whiteboard as the static blackboard. Blended with traditional methods, replacing some of them, e-learning allows a new relationship with learners to develop. It takes them beyond the confines of the traditional classroom, extending collaboration, and enabling teachers to bring new resources into their teaching, culled from a world of digital libraries. Teachers can enrich their lessons by taking pupils, through online conferencing or web-cams, to authentic environments from wildlife parks and museums to overseas classrooms.

What will ICT do for leaders?

Learners, parents or carers will increasingly expect electronic information and contact. With good systems, school, college and university leaders will find it easier to offer flexibility, and tailor their courses to what their students want. Adult learners increasingly expect easy online access to their course resources, timetables, achievement records and their tutors. School pupils and their parents are beginning to expect the same. Parents want a shared role in their children's education and development – to

access the syllabus for the term, to see what they are working on now, what's coming up, and how much homework is expected.

What will it do for employers and the private sector?

Technology also allows a new relationship between education and employers. School leavers will have an electronic portfolio showing their achievements and their best work – giving a clearer insight into what they can do in the workplace. ICT infused throughout the curriculum at all levels of education will generate school leavers and graduates better equipped with the skills needed for 21st-century employment. New partnerships will give employees easy access to online learning where and when they need it. Industry can more easily connect to the research base through virtual science parks, not restricted to location, but focused around interest and need. Private companies have long used technology to modernise their training methods. The public sector can learn from their experience.

When will we get there?

The future we describe is already happening in the most go-ahead places. We must learn from the best so that all can benefit. We can only harness the new technologies to our ambitions if we are clear about what we want, and how best to use ICT to achieve it.

We want to use ICT to build a society where everybody has the opportunity to develop their potential. We will ensure that all those working in our education and children's services are able to use the technology well. From that baseline, we can effect a genuine transformation of educational provision in the future.

What does it mean for learners?

As a learner, you should have:

More ways to learn: the chance to develop the skills you need for participating fully in a technology-rich society. Along with listening and reading, you will be spending more time learning in groups, working with other learners, being creative, learning through challenging, game-like activities and materials that adjust to the level and pace appropriate to you, and with clear personal goals that you help to set.

More subjects to choose from: you should have access to subjects taught through partnerships with schools, colleges, or universities, or other sources of adult learning, through carefully designed materials, with expert support online, and networking with your peer group, in your community or workplace, choosing from a wide range of topics provided by accredited learning and training providers.

More flexible study: you will have more choice about where, when and how you study, making it easier for you to create your own mix between studying in a place with other learners, learning at work, learning at home, and learning online.

Easier ways to try things out: if you're not sure you're interested in further learning, there will be online access to informal tasters, linked to leisure or domestic activities, enabling you to progress to the next stage by means of highly motivating short modules, as and when you wish.

A personal online learning space: where you can store electronically everything related to your learning and achievements, course resources, assignments, research, plan your next steps, and build links for professional advice and support. And being online, it will be accessible from home, from school, and, in the longer term, from each new organisation as you progress.

Help to move on: you can find out online what courses are available, and which ones might suit you best, with online questionnaires to assess where you are now, where you want to be, and how to get there.

We need to make sure our learners can receive these opportunities. Moving toward making this a reality requires intervention and action. We are building on a great deal of strength and existing experience in all sectors. The Becta Review has documented this (Review 2005 – Evidence on the progress of ICT in education), as well as the issues we need to address. There is a gap between strong and weak ICT use in all sectors. Our challenge is to ensure that every institution is maximising its potential for good practice in e-learning. With our partners, we have determined priority actions at system level that we will drive across all our strategies, and the actions that are specific to the needs of the four sectors.

■ The above information is from the e-Strategy 'Harnessing Technology: Transforming learning and children's services', a report from the Department for Education and Skills – for more information visit their website at www.dfes.gov.uk

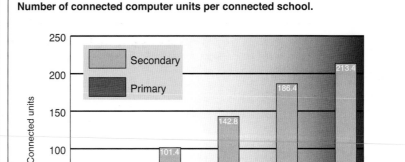

Internet accessibility in schools

Number of connected computer units per connected school.

Source: BESA

Old-fashioned education?

Pupils make more progress in 3Rs 'without aid of computers'

By John Clare,
Education Editor

The less pupils use computers at school and at home, the better they do in international tests of literacy and maths, the largest study of its kind says today (21 March 2005).

The findings raise questions over the Government's decision, announced by Gordon Brown in the Budget last week, to spend another £1.5 billion on school computers, in addition to the £2.5 billion it has already spent.

> *The evidence so far suggests that computer use in schools does not seem to contribute substantially to students' learning of basic skills such as maths or reading*

Mr Brown said: 'The teaching and educational revolution is no longer blackboards and chalk, it is computers and electronic whiteboards.'

However, the study, published by the Royal Economic Society, said: 'Despite numerous claims by politicians and software vendors to the contrary, the evidence so far suggests that computer use in schools does not seem to contribute substantially to students' learning of basic skills such as maths or reading.'

Indeed, the more pupils used computers, the worse they performed, said Thomas Fuchs and Ludger Wossmann of Munich University.

Their report also noted that being able to use a computer at work – one of the justifications for devoting so much teaching time to ICT (information and communications technology) – had no greater impact on employability or wage levels than being able to use a telephone or a pencil.

The researchers analysed the achievements and home backgrounds of 100,000 15-year-olds in 31 countries taking part in the PISA (Programme for International Student Assessment) study in 2000 for the Organisation for Economic Cooperation and Development.

PISA, to the British and many other governments' satisfaction, claimed that the more pupils used computers the better they did. It even suggested those with more than one computer at home were a year ahead of those who had none.

The study found this conclusion 'highly misleading' because computer availability at home is linked to other family-background characteristics, in the same way computer availability at school is strongly linked to availability of other resources.

Once those influences were eliminated, the relationship between use of computers and performance in maths and literacy tests was reduced to zero, showing how 'careless interpretations can lead to patently false conclusions'.

The more access pupils had to computers at home, the lower they scored in tests, partly because they diverted attention from homework.

Pupils tended to do worse in schools generously equipped with computers, apparently because computerised instruction replaced more effective forms of teaching.

The Government says computers are the key to 'personalised learning' and computers should be 'embedded' in the teaching of every subject.

Ruth Kelly, the Education Secretary, has said: 'We must move the thinking about ICT from being an add-on to being an integral part of the way we teach and learn.'

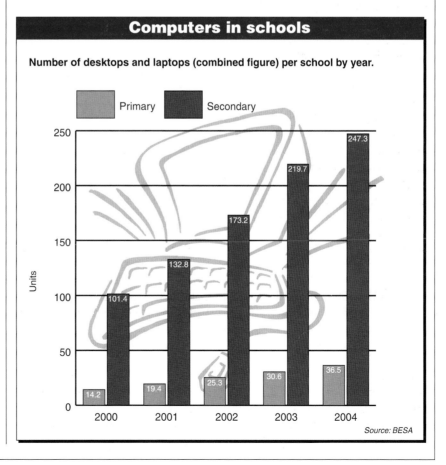

Computers in schools

Number of desktops and laptops (combined figure) per school by year.

Primary   Secondary

Year	Primary	Secondary
2000	14.2	101.4
2001	19.4	132.8
2002	25.3	173.2
2003	30.6	219.7
2004	36.5	247.3

Units

Source: BESA

Internet to change the face of banking in five years

We may love to hate our bank, but in the next five years the future of the local high street bank branch faces yet more debate. More than seven in ten people (77%) say they will do their banking and pay their bills (72%) online in the next five years, according to new figures from Pipex, the leading UK provider of broadband services.

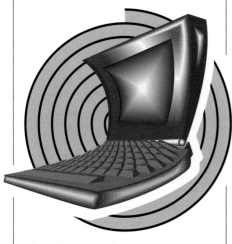

With more than half (53%) of Britain's homes now online and with a third of those enjoying a broadband connection, the new poll suggests that broadband will drive a revived explosion in Internet usage, which in turn will change the way we live our daily lives.

In the latest in a series of probes into broadband services, Pipex asked a GB representative sample of 1,900 Britons what they expected to use the Internet for within the next five years.

Key findings

- More than 60% of the population will use their home computer to do a range of daily tasks – such as storing photos (71 per cent) and talking to friends in sound and pictures (65 per cent). Further, 72 per cent will pay their bills online and a massive 77 per cent of people will shun long queues and do their day-to-day banking online.

More than 60% of the population will use their home computer to do a range of daily tasks – such as storing photos (71 per cent) and talking to friends in sound and pictures (65 per cent)

- The home PC will also become invaluable in keeping people informed. In addition to the majority of people using their home PC to keep up with the latest news, 45 per cent of Brits will turn to the Web for medical advice – a reaction, perhaps, against long NHS waiting lists.
- Looking at bigger lifestyle issues, more than four in ten people will use the Web to find a new house (44 per cent), and liberate themselves from a working commute (42 per cent) by working from home. Around one in 13 busy Brits will even use their home PC to find true love (7%).
- The Pipex findings also shatter the myth that home computing is a male pastime. There is strong use of the home PC by women and in some instances they are set to steal the march on men, suggesting mums and wives will continue to wear the trousers at home. For example, women are more likely than men to use the Internet to: look for houses (45 per cent to 43 per cent) or to shop for clothes (40 per cent to 36 per cent) or food (40 per cent to 32 per cent).
- Whilst all age groups want to use the net to save time on mundane banking and bills, it is people under 30 that are driving many of the new trends. Young people are those most likely to make active use of auction sites to find bargains (61 per cent), to house hunt (65 per cent), to store music instead of buying CDs (66 per cent) and to say they intend to work from home in the future (56 per cent). For young people the retail experience from banking to shoe shopping is an online experience – and this is set to become the norm for Britain by 2010.

Regional highlights

- A north / south divide emerges when it comes to shopping, people in the north proving savvier and more switched on to sniffing out an online bargain (40 per cent to 32 per cent in the south).
- Londoners were those most likely to want to work from home (54 per cent), to escape antiquated trains and the overcrowded tube.
- Finally, despite the overcrowded Capital it also seems to be the place of lonely hearts. Londoners are twice as likely as the national average to look for love over the Web (14 per cent).

Dominic Crolla, GM of Broadband, Pipex, commented: 'Despite the hype of the dot com bubble some years ago, home use of the Internet has rocketed in the last few years and broadband is behind this renaissance. In addition to providing a faster service, broadband frees up people's leisure time. As the pioneer of broadband in the UK, Pipex has tailored a number of packages to meet the varying needs of the public. Broadband is cheap and will change the way we work rest and play by 2010.'

- The above information is from Pipex – visit www.pipex.net or see page 41 for their address details.

© Pipex

The digital divide

Government announces new plans to close digital divide

National challenge for region to 'go digital'

A seven-point action plan to close the digital divide, including a national digital challenge for a region to give universal online access to local public services by 2008, was unveiled by the Prime Minister and Secretary of State for Trade and Industry today (1 April 2005).

There is evidence in the UK of a digital divide, with some groups largely excluded from benefiting from access to the Internet for a variety of reasons including cost, lack of confidence or skills in using computers, and relevance.

The seven-point plan includes:

- A 'digital challenge' prize to be awarded to a local authority and its partners to give universal online access to local public services. The winner will have the opportunity to demonstrate the ability to transform service delivery through using technology to deliver modern services for modern citizens;
- A commitment to give all students the opportunity to access ICT at home through a low cost national laptop and home PC leasing scheme. Ensuring that ICT is embedded in education to improve the quality of learning for all and equip children with skills increasingly essential in the workplace. All learners will have their own virtual learning space where they can store and access their work;
- Working with the IT industry to create the safest possible online environment, backed by the police, charities, and the industry. The Home Office is announcing today the establishment of a multi-agency national Internet safety centre to deter criminals targeting children for Internet crime and reassure parents. And we will work with the banking industry to make

that sector a market leader in terms of online authentication;

- Further steps towards closing the digital divide by building on the network of UK Online centres and other communal access points giving adult learners the support, incentives and skills they need to make the most of ICT;
- Creating the right environment to stimulate broadband content, particularly in public procurement. This will set out guidance on broadband content procurement by the public sector;
- A cross-government focus on public service delivery transformed by modern technology and a strategy for achieving that. As part of that strategy, the Government will consider how it moves its business to a wholly digital environment where it is appropriate and cost effective;
- Asking Ofcom to include in their regulatory strategy for the broadband market a forward look on the prospects for home broadband take-up, with a particular focus on uptake amongst the more disadvantaged.

Patricia Hewitt said: 'This Government has invested in a range of groundbreaking programmes to transform the UK from a poor relation to a digitally rich nation in just a few years.

'That's a great success but the job is not done.

'We aim to make the UK a world leader in digital excellence with public services that are even more responsive, personalised and efficient than the leading companies that have successfully deployed the Internet to serve their customers.

'We are committed to ending the digital divide for families with children, and the Prime Minister's Strategy Unit and DTI, in partnership with industry, aim to make the UK a world leader in digital excellence and the first nation to close the digital divide.'

The Government is committed to improving accessibility to technology for the digitally excluded and ease of use for the disabled.

UK businesses are amongst the most sophisticated users of ICT in the world.

By the end of this summer, 99 per cent of the population will have access to broadband and the rate of broadband adoption exceeds the rates of adoption seen for mains electricity, colour TV and mobile phones.

- The above information is from the Department of Trade and Industry. For more information visit www.dti.gov.uk

© Crown Copyright

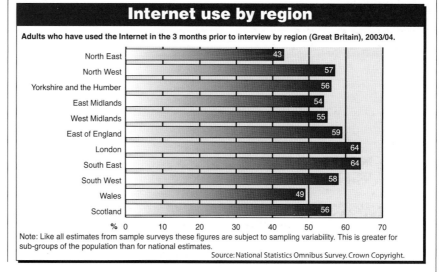

Internet use by region

Adults who have used the Internet in the 3 months prior to interview by region (Great Britain), 2003/04.

Region	%
North East	43
North West	57
Yorkshire and the Humber	56
East Midlands	54
West Midlands	55
East of England	59
London	64
South East	64
South West	58
Wales	49
Scotland	56

Note: Like all estimates from sample surveys these figures are subject to sampling variability. This is greater for sub-groups of the population than for national estimates.

Source: National Statistics Omnibus Survey. Crown Copyright.

Ten years of Cyberia

More a meeting place than a coffee shop, the Internet café is 10 years old. Nic Fleming reports

It may come as a shock to those who can't tell their USB ports from their wireless ethernets, but the Internet café is 10 years old today (1 September 2004).

What started as the brainwave of a homesick Polish student has become a fixture of high streets from Swansea to Timbuktu.

From a modest beginning in London the Internet café is now familiar all over the world.

There are now more than 20,000 Internet cafés across the world, with their customers using them as something close to a post office, shopping centre, newspaper and library rolled into one.

Eva Pascoe, a Polish psychology student, opened Café Cyberia, the world's first Internet café, in Whitfield Street, central London, on Sept 1, 1994.

To celebrate the concept's 10th birthday, Yahoo! Mail today publishes its inaugural Internet café awards.

James Bilefield, from Yahoo!, said: 'The Internet café concept is as fresh and as relevant today as it was 10 years ago.

'It's now second nature for people on the move to use the local Internet café to keep up with the news from home and to tell friends and family where they have been.

'Many Internet cafés also provide an essential service for the community and, in the developing world, a place where people can learn from the Internet and communicate with others around the globe.'

More than 1,000 nominations were received from travellers who visited Internet cafés in 111 countries. They are listed in *The Rough Guide to the World's Best Internet Cafés*, an e-book [an electronic book available on the Internet] that can be downloaded at www.yahoo.co.uk.

The cafés were entered into one of five categories: Most Remote, Most Unusual, Most Stylish, Best UK and a special Life Saver category for those that were there in the traveller's hour of need.

Ms Pascoe was writing her PhD at City University in London in 1994 when she first struck on the idea of an Internet café.

She said: 'I was spending a long time away from my family, working on my PhD. I had access to email, but at the time the Internet was mainly an academic service. One day I was sitting having a cup of coffee and it occurred to me it that it would be fun to have a drink and bring my laptop to the coffee shop to send emails while having a break from work.

'We figured out that we could actually put a permanent PC connection in a café and link it to the Internet.

'Three months later we set up in Whitfield Street. The only problem was that my coffee machine could only make one cappuccino every two minutes, so the shop was full of people who were lining up to use the Internet and demanding their coffees faster than I could provide them.'

There are now more than 20,000 Internet cafés across the world, with their customers using them as something close to a post office, shopping centre, newspaper and library rolled into one

Ms Pascoe invested in new equipment for Café Cyberia, and soon attracted investment from the likes of Maurice Saatchi and Mick Jagger.

Cyberia cafés later opened in many other cities as far afield as Paris, Tokyo, Bangkok and Manila.

© *Telegraph Group Limited, London 2004*

Email to all staff . . . ◆ ◆ ◆

. . . how about getting on with your work?

More than a quarter of employees spend an hour or more a day on personal emails when they should be working, it emerged yesterday (15 Feb 2005).

In a business with 100 staff, that amounts to more than 1,200 working days being lost over the course of a year.

Such a firm would have to take on five extra staff to make up for lost productivity.

Experts say many employees are taking liberties and using their workplace computers simply as a way of making arrangements for their social life.

They believe the true amount of time workers waste could be even higher, because the figures only assessed time spent using email for personal reasons, not time spent surfing the Internet.

Some 4,500 workers from the UK, Germany and the US were questioned for a survey by the Internet security firm Clearswift.

Overall, 36 per cent said they spent an hour or more a day at work writing or reading personal emails – although the figure for the UK alone was lower at 27 per cent. A further 22 per cent of British staff spent half an hour per day on them while 38 per cent spent 15 minutes.

Only one worker in ten said they never used the company email system for personal reasons.

More than three-quarters of workers questioned said their boss would be 'unconcerned' if they knew how much time their employees were wasting.

But Ruth Lea, director of the Centre for Policy Studies think-tank, disagreed.

She said: 'I think an hour or more a day on personal emails is taking the mickey.

'It is really way over the top and it is abusing a position of trust.

'It's almost got to the point now where some people go to work to extend their home or social lives.

'I am deeply sceptical of the idea that any boss would be happy with that situation. I think a lot of them would be furious.'

The survey also revealed that workers in IT departments were most likely to spend time at work chatting online.

They waste nearly 17 days every year on personal emails, compared with an average of 13 days for other British workers.

David Guyatt, chief executive officer at Clearswift, said productivity rates could be significantly improved if firms got tough on employees using email for personal reasons.

He said: 'In a typical 100-person company in the UK, for example, the survey shows that 1,258 working days each year are lost because people are using corporate email systems for non-company purposes.

'That's equivalent to around five new full-time staff.

'Added to other issues such as loss of confidential information, inappropriate email use leads to personal harassment, compliance challenges, spam and viruses.

'Companies need to set the ground rules with employees on web and email usage through clear policies to ensure productivity does not suffer.'

Trust in online resources

Information from MORI

More people use the Internet than do not, and half (49%) say they know at least a fair amount about the world wide web, according to new research from MORI. The project, for the Common Information Environment (CIE) group, found the reputation of an organisation and the trustworthiness of the content of websites are important factors in determining people's attitudes towards online information resources.

A majority of users (80%) access the Internet at home, and more than half (51%) say it is their preferred information source. Eight in 10 of those who have ever used the web say they have used it to search for specific information, and it is websites of more established organisations such as museums, libraries and archives which are more likely to be trusted by people. This is particularly in comparison to more commercial websites such as utility companies, travel agencies and Internet-only retail companies.

Non-users of the Internet fall into two broad categories: those for whom little would need to change to encourage them to get online cheaper ICT costs, easier access, better awareness about what is available on the web and, importantly, more confidence about using it and a 'hardcore' (amounting to approximately 15% of the population as a whole) whose non-use is genuinely related to indifference rather than access, cost or other issues.

Technical details

The MORI Social Research Institute carried out 2,004 interviews with members of the UK general public aged 16+, face to face, in-home between 13 October and 18 November 2004. This included 1,393 respondents who have ever used the web (1,265 current and 128 lapsed users) and 585 who have never used it.

Information wants to be liquid

By Jason Walsh

The web as we know it was invented by a British academic working in Switzerland. Is a Nordic academic working in Britain about to redefine it for ever?

Frode Hegland, a researcher at University College London, wants to change the basic structure of information on the net.

Hegland's project, Liquid Information, is kinda like Wikipedia meets hypertext. In Hegland's web, all documents are editable, and every word is a potential hyperlink.

Hegland is based at University College London's Interaction Centre and collaborates with Doug Engelbart, inventor of the mouse. Engelbart refers to Hegland's project as 'the next stage of the web'.

Hegland's idea is simple – he plans to move beyond the basic hypertext linking of the web, and change every word into a 'hyperword'. Instead of one or two links in a document, every single word becomes a link. Further, every link can point to more than one place, pulling up all kinds of background context from the web as a whole.

Click on a politician's name and find out who donated to his or her campaign. Click on a town name in a news story and find out what else has happened there.

'We feel that a large part of the history of technology, digital and otherwise, has been about the production of information,' Hegland said. 'It's time to focus on consumption, to help people navigate through information and get relevant information into their heads.'

The project started in 2003, but Hegland has been thinking about interfaces and information for a long time. 'I've been working on these ideas since 1991,' he said. Then the web happened.

When Tim Berners-Lee first developed the web at CERN, he intended it to be an interactive back-and-forth, akin to projects like the

Wikipedia. But in the monolithic web of today, you're either a consumer or a producer, never both at the same time.

Liquid Information takes Berners-Lee's ideas and runs with them. Hegland's experimental system is geared toward allowing users – not just writers and editors – to make connections. Instead of just viewing websites, readers can change the way information is presented, or relate it to other information elsewhere on the web.

The Liquid Information project's homepage proudly states, 'You can think of this project as an effort to turn web browsers into web readers.'

Currently, the project offers a basic demo: a live version of the CNN website, where hovering over any word causes a context-sensitive menu to appear.

The menu offers a series of options – users can Google the word, highlight it, get a dictionary definition of it or show only paragraphs which contain it, among other things.

But this is only the beginning, Hegland insisted. The Liquid Information project has much grander aims. Eventually, users would be allowed to process information in

any way imaginable. For example, if readers prefer *The New York Times* to Wired News, or Fox News to AlterNet, they will be able to add subsets of preferred sites to hyperword menus.

'Users will need to be educated and some people see this as a problem, but people are pretty smart,' said Hegland. 'The days of baby steps when everything is shown to users are over... Today, the web is a collection of handmade, one-way links. That's it as far as interactivity is concerned... Legibility is important, but legibility with interactivity, or deep legibility, is crucial to help us follow connections, explicit or otherwise.'

'There's plenty of information out there and Google gives us the tiniest fraction of an idea of what's possible,' said Bruce Horn, the veteran programmer behind the original Macintosh file browser, the Finder. '(But) data is not information, which is not knowledge, which is not wisdom. If people were able to find out things quickly and easily, for example how people in politics had been voting, they'd be able to make better decisions.'

Horn said Google is moving in a parallel direction. The search giant's recent moves into desktop search, the scanning of library books and the purchasing of old Usenet posts point toward Google's view of the Internet as a 'network operating system', dedicated to information.

But Horn said Hegland's motives are rather different.

'This isn't about being the next Google,' Horn said. 'The goal is to try and change the world for the better – not necessarily to make a ton of money.'

Opportunities and risks go hand in hand

Information from the Internet Watch Foundation

Children and young people who make the best use of the Internet also encounter more risks online.

This is one of the main findings from a two-year research study by the London School of Economics and Political Science (LSE).

The UK Children Go Online (UKCGO) project involved a series of focus group discussions and then a national survey of 1,511 9- to 19-year-olds around the UK, together with their parents, in order to examine young people's Internet use in detail. The research is funded by the Economic and Social Research Council under the e-Society Programme.

> *Restricting children and young people's Internet use reduces the risks but also carries a cost because it reduces their opportunities online*

The report compares more skilled Internet users with beginners.

Professor Sonia Livingstone and co-author Dr Magdalena Bober found that:

1. Children and young people who are more skilled at using the Internet take up more online opportunities than beginners – such as using the Internet for learning, communicating with friends or seeking advice.
2. It is the skilled youngsters, more than the beginners, who are likely to encounter online risks – such as bullying, online porn or privacy risks.
3. Increasing online opportunities also increases the risks.
4. Those who manage to avoid the risks seem to do so by making only a narrow and unadventurous use of the Internet.

Sonia Livingstone, Professor of Social Psychology at the LSE, said: 'This points up the dilemma that parents and other regulators face. Restricting children and young people's Internet use reduces the risks but also carries a cost because it reduces their opportunities online.

'It is of concern that even the most skilled young people are not avoiding online risks. If we want to make sure that in five years' time young people aren't at greater risk online, more effort is needed to make the Internet safer for them.'

The research raises the question what parents can do to ensure their children are making the best use of the Internet.

Professor Livingstone said: 'Parents who employ supportive practices, rather than simply restricting Internet use, increase their children's online skills and, as a result, increase their opportunities. This includes asking the child what they are doing online, keeping an eye on the screen, helping them online, staying in the same room and going online together. However, this may not reduce online risks.'

Schools also have a role to play. Co-author of the report, Magdalena Bober, said: 'Many pupils have already received some lessons on how to use the Internet. However, nearly one in three have not. Schools should provide more specific guidance on Internet safety, searching and reliability of websites, especially to the younger children (9-11 years) and the oldest (18-19 years), who are less likely to have received such lessons.'

The research also found that:
1. Beginners lack searching and critical skills and so are more distrustful of online content than skilled users.

2. However, skilled users don't show blind trust. Rather, they are better at searching and more able to find reliable websites, for example by checking information across several sites.
3. Overall, only one in three 9- to 19-year-old Internet users have been taught how to decide if the information they find online is reliable and can be trusted.

Stephen Carrick-Davies, CEO of Childnet International, one of the report sponsors, said: 'This research reminds us that supporting and protecting children online is a complex business, and there are no simple "one size fits all" solutions. If we want to expand children's online opportunities, we have to recognise that even the most advanced and confident young user will still be open to risks and dangers online.

We have to recognise that even the most advanced and confident young user will still be open to risks and dangers online

---

'Developing critical net-literacy skills in young people is therefore crucial, and this has to involve parents helping children and having meaningful interaction about the Internet. It is also vital that teachers really understand how children are interacting on the Internet outside of the classroom, where it is generally filtered, protected and supervised. This is where more work and support is needed if we are to ensure that children are truly life-literate as well as net-literate.'

■ The above information is reprinted with kind permission from the Internet Watch Foundation – visit www.iwf.org.uk for more or see page 41 for address details.

© IWF

The Internet

Information from the Internet Watch Foundation

The Internet is a world-wide network that provides electronic connection between computers enabling them to communicate with each other.

Global

Online information and websites can be created, hosted and accessed from all over the world, by anyone, at any time.

There is a vast amount of data available on virtually every subject imaginable and there is no doubt that the world wide web has changed the way the world communicates.

The global nature of the Internet means it is very difficult to formally regulate it in the same way as other means of mass communication such as television, radio or offline publications.

There is no central international body that monitors or approves Internet content before it appears online.

Content – use and abuse

A substantial amount of Internet content available provides consumers with an interesting, positive and educational experience, but because of the freedom offered by the Internet, combined with this lack of direct governance by a central body, there is always the potential for misuse.

The proliferation of indecent images of children being sexually abused has been a concern for many years. Whilst such images have, unfortunately, always existed, Internet technologies have, without doubt, allowed a far wider dissemination of this type of content across the world.

Boundaries and regulation

Because the Internet is not confined within any national or even international boundary, the way that countries around the globe deal with regulation of Internet content is to apply their own legislation to an Internet transaction that takes place in their country.

Obviously, this creates disparity in laws governing online behaviour and the control of Internet content around the world.

For example, images which are illegal to view in the UK may not be illegal to view in Japan.

Legal framework

Each country has a responsibility to develop their own legislation that they can apply to Internet content within their jurisdiction.

Self or co-regulation through public reporting

As Internet use in the UK grew and developed, it became apparent that to protect UK ISPs' service from being abused through the posting and hosting of illegal child abuse images and in turn, protect UK Internet consumers from being exposed to these images an independent, intermediary online reporting mechanism was needed.

This would provide a notification procedure for UK ISPs who would be alerted to any illegal content on their services, allowing them to then remove it. It would also allow consumers a free public support service and offer them reassurance when using the Internet.

To be successful, this model would require co-operation and partnerships across the Internet industry, the police and the Government.

■ The above information is reprinted with kind permission from the Internet Watch Foundation – visit www.iwf.org.uk for more information or see page 41 for address details.

© IWF

The Internet – it's a real world out there!

Parents' Internet safety facts

It can be a tough job keeping up to date with kids these days. Just when we thought we were doing OK and could set the video recorder, along comes the Internet. Suddenly we have a new piece of technology, new language and new challenges for us parents! This guide will help you understand the online safety issues and gives practical help as you talk to your children about their Internet use with the SMART Safety Tips.

But my kids know more than I do!

Many adults can feel intimidated in using the Internet and are baffled by some of the terms and technology. While it is true that many children may have better technical skills than you, children still need parental advice and protection in using this new tool. After all, you can teach your children the importance of wearing a seat belt in a car without understanding how the car engine works!

So what are the dangers?

The Internet is like bringing a city into your living room: there are the exciting places for children to go and enjoy but also lots of places where you wouldn't want your children to go unsupervised! The main dangers for children can be grouped into:

- Potential CONTACT – from someone online who may wish to harm them. Children must re-learn the 'stranger=danger' rule in a new context and never give out personal details or meet alone with anyone they've contacted via the Internet.
- Inappropriate CONTENT – keep an eye on the material your children are looking at and agree the ground rules about where your children go and how they behave.

Childnet
International

- Excessive COMMERCIALISM and advertising which invades your child's privacy. Encourage your children not to fill out forms which ask for lots of personal details.

Can't I just use a filter?

Filtering software can help to block a lot of inappropriate material but they are not 100% effective and are no substitute for good parental involvement. Internet use at school is generally filtered, supervised and safe. But many children use the Net at friends' homes, Internet cafes, libraries and youth clubs where there may be no filters and little super-vision. It's therefore important to help educate your children about how to behave online and discuss prob-lems which they may have. It helps to keep the computer in a family room – not tucked away in a bedroom.

What about mobile phones?

The issues about being careful online apply equally to mobile telephones. The next generation of mobiles and handheld devices will have more and more Internet facilities on them. It is very important to encourage your children not to give out their mobile numbers to strangers or people they cannot trust completely. Talk about the sort of text messages your children are receiving and sending.

Stick to the positive

Encourage your children to stick to the fun and positive sites on the Net that reinforce their interests. Just as you look out for good TV programmes for children take the time to find the best and most useful websites for you and your family.

Communicating your issues

If you start by telling your child never to do something most children will ask 'why not?' and then try to find out! Discussing the potential dangers with your children therefore needs care and sensitivity and involves helping them to see for themselves how they might get into difficulty. Most children will respond more positively if you encourage them to be SMART or 'Cool' on the Internet rather than giving them a list of 'Dos and don'ts'! The following SMART TIPS have been written especially for children aged 8-14 years.

- SAFE – Staying safe involves being careful and not giving out your name, address, mobile phone no., school name or password to people online.
- MEETING someone you have contacted in cyberspace can be dangerous. Only do so with your parent's/carer's permission, and then when they can be present.
- ACCEPTING emails or opening files from people you don't really know or trust can get you into trouble – they may contain viruses or nasty messages.
- RELIABLE – Someone online may be lying about who they are, and information you find on the Internet may not be reliable.
- TELL your parent or carer if someone or something makes you feel uncomfortable or worried.

- Information from Childnet International – visit www.childnet-int.org or see page 41 for address details.

© *Childnet*

Parents must act on online safety advice

Industry research shows lack of parental action to improve children's online safety

Only eight per cent of parents with children aged five to fifteen have implemented five of the most simple and important child safety guidelines.

A survey conducted by ICM Research (ICM) on behalf of the Internet Services Providers' Association (ISPA) – the UK's leading Internet trade association – has aroused concern that many parents are not acting on safety advice to help to protect their children on the Internet.

The study considered parents with children between five and fifteen and Internet access at home.

Jessica Hendrie-Liano, the Chair of the ISPA Council, said, 'Protecting children on the Internet must be a joint effort between the Internet industry, the Government and its agencies and parents. Many ISPs offer online safety features such as web and spam filters and parents should take advantage of these facilities.'

Mrs Hendrie-Liano continued, 'Although there is a great deal of awareness about online safety hazards in the UK, this research highlights a worrying lack of action by many parents to help children have a safer online experience. Only eight per cent of parents with children aged five to fifteen have implemented five of the most simple and important child safety guidelines. Parents should ensure that their children use the Internet in a communal room, offer their children regular reminders of online safety rules, know who their children are talking to online, surf the net with their children and ensure that the computer their children use to access the Internet has functioning online safety software.'

Children should use the Internet in a communal area of the home

Nearly two out of five (38 per cent) parents allow their children to use the Internet in a private room.

The study showed that parents who ensure that their children use the Internet in a communal room, such as the lounge, most frequently offer Internet safety advice to children.

Mrs Hendrie-Liano said, 'Not only is it easier to offer children safety advice more frequently, by keeping the computer in a communal area it is also much easier to monitor what your children are viewing online.'

Parents should regularly remind children of online safety rules

Only two-fifths of parents (41 per cent) give regular reminders to their children about online safety rules.

Nearly one-third of parents (28 per cent) have never spoken to their child about giving out personal information such as their home address, telephone numbers or passwords on the Internet.

Only two-fifths of parents (41 per cent) give regular reminders to their children about online safety rules

---

Mrs Hendrie-Liano recommended, 'Parents should offer their children regular reminders of online safety rules. In particular, children should be taught not to give out personal information such as their home address, school, telephone numbers or passwords on the Internet. Although the vast majority of Internet users are honest in their intentions, children in particular must understand that people on the Internet may not always be who they say they are.'

Parents should know who their child is talking to online

As many as one in eight parents (13 per cent) do not know if their child uses chat rooms. Of the 26 per cent

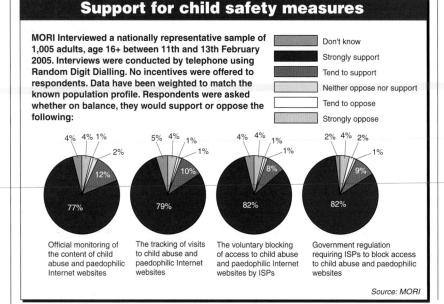

Support for child safety measures

MORI Interviewed a nationally representative sample of 1,005 adults, age 16+ between 11th and 13th February 2005. Interviews were conducted by telephone using Random Digit Dialling. No incentives were offered to respondents. Data have been weighted to match the known population profile. Respondents were asked whether on balance, they would support or oppose the following:

Don't know
Strongly support
Tend to support
Neither oppose nor support
Tend to oppose
Strongly oppose

4% 4% 1% 2% 12% 77%
Official monitoring of the content of child abuse and paedophilic Internet websites

5% 4% 1% 1% 10% 79%
The tracking of visits to child abuse and paedophilic Internet websites

4% 4% 1% 1% 8% 82%
The voluntary blocking of access to child abuse and paedophilic Internet websites by ISPs

2% 4% 2% 1% 9% 82%
Government regulation requiring ISPs to block access to child abuse and paedophilic websites

Source: MORI

of parents who know that their children do use chat rooms, 65 per cent admit to not knowing their children's online friends.

ISPA recommends that parents should talk to their children about chat rooms. It is important that they talk to their children about who they are meeting online, and ensure that children are wary of strangers.

Mrs Hendrie-Liano said, 'If children are chatting online, parents should make sure they are only visiting moderated chat rooms. Even then, they should know who their online friends are, just as they would know their child's friends in the offline world.'

Parents should go online with their children

Although 63 per cent of parents frequently use the Internet with their children at home, nearly one in four (23 per cent) parents have never used the Internet with their child.

Surfing can be a family activity. ISPA urges parents to use the Internet together with their child, talk about what the child likes and discuss any problems that might be encountered.

Mrs Hendrie-Liano said, 'Parents must remember that just like the offline world, the online world has its hazards. Parents should empower themselves to set their children's boundaries. Just as parents look out for quality TV programmes for children, they should also take the time to find the best and most useful sites for them and their family.'

Family computers should have functioning safety software

ISPA recommends that parents should explore the safety services and software available from their ISP and should consider these features when selecting their ISP.

One-third of parents (32 per cent) have not enabled basic safety features such as web and spam filtering solutions.

Of the 68 per cent of parents that have enabled such safety features, one in eight of them do not know if they have done so correctly.

Mrs Hendrie-Liano said, 'Online safety software can help to protect your children and your computer.

However, no amount of software can replace parental supervision. Children must also be taught not to open emails and attachments or download files from strangers.'

UK kids far from Internet addicts

Parents are noticing that children are only online for an average of four hours 35 minutes per week. Only one in eight children are on the Internet for more than ten hours per week. This is a good indicator that children are keeping up their other interests.

Mrs Hendrie-Liano said, 'It's hard to dispute that the Internet offers a great resource to help children learn, create and connect with other children worldwide. Families generally realise the enormous educational and social benefits of the Internet.'

The UK is currently leading the world in the development of a safer Internet

ISPA created one of the world's first codes of practice for providers of Internet services. UK ISPs created one of the earliest self-regulatory 'notice and takedown' procedures in the world, whereby ISPs can remove unlawful content when they have knowledge that it is present on their system.

The Internet Watch Foundation (IWF) was the first organisation in the world created to address illegal online content – it was established and is funded by the UK Internet industry. Less than one per cent of the illegal content the IWF is notified about is hosted on the UK Internet. The majority of such content is hosted in Eastern Europe and the USA.

ISPA has also worked with the Government to create the world's first guidelines for providers of chat services.

The Home Office Task Force for Child Protection on the Internet is a joint initiative between the Internet industry, the Government, the Police and children's charities. ISPA has contributed to the ongoing success of the thinkuknow.co.uk website and the 'Keep Your Child Safe on the Internet' leaflet campaign.

Mrs Hendrie-Liano concluded, 'Children's safety online should be a shared responsibility between the Internet industry, Government and parents. Without the involvement and action of parents and carers, much of the Government's and Internet industry's efforts are squandered. This research underlines the fact that parents must act on Internet safety advice to offer their children a safer online experience.'

■ The above information is from Internet Service Providers' Association – visit www.ispa.org.uk or see page 41 for address details.

© ISPA

Internet safety by age

Information from http://kids.getnetwise.org

2 to about 4

This is the age of 'lapware' when children start interacting with the computer in the presence of a parent or sibling. There are numerous activities and sites that are likely to be appropriate for this age group but, in most cases, it makes sense for the parent and child to be exploring together. This is not just a safety issue, but also a way to assure that the child has a pleasant experience, and to help build bonds between the child and the older person who is surfing the Internet with them.

> *Encourage them to explore a variety of websites, not just one or two of their favourites*

Starting at about age 3, some children can benefit by having a bit more independence so that they can explore, experience discoveries, and make mistakes on their own. That doesn't mean that they should be given free access. It's probably best for parents to choose the Web sites they visit and not let them leave those sites on their own. You don't necessarily need to stand over them or sit with them the entire time that they're in a known safe site.

4 to about 7

Children begin to explore on their own, but it's still important for parents to be in very close touch with their children as they explore the Net. When your child's at this age you should consider restricting her access only to sites that you have visited and feel are appropriate. For help with this matter, you can consider using one of the pre-screened websites in GetNetWise, as well as child-safe search engines.

At this age it's important that kids experience positive results from sites that can enhance their discovery. The issue here isn't so much avoiding dangerous sites, but making sure they are visiting sites that don't frustrate them or lead them down blind alleys.

7 to about 10

During this period, children begin looking outside the family for social validation and information. This is when peer pressure begins to become an issue for many kids. It's also a time when kids are looking for more independence from parents, according to psychologist Richard Toft. During these years, children should be encouraged to do a bit more exploring on their own, but that doesn't mean that the parents shouldn't be close at hand. Just as you wouldn't send children at this age to a movie by themselves, it's important to be with them – or at least nearby – when they explore the Net. For this age group, consider putting the computer in a kitchen area, family room, den, or other areas where the child has access to Mum or Dad while using the computer. That way, they can be 'independent' but not alone.

Also, consider using a filtering program or restricting them to sites that you locate via a child-safe search engine. Another option for this age group is a child-friendly browser.

When your child is at this stage, you need to be concerned not so much about what he's doing online

and with the PC as how long he's spending on the PC. Be sure that his time on the computer and the Internet doesn't take away from all his other activities. Kids need variety, and it's not a good idea for them to be spending all of their time on any single activity, even reading books. One way to deal with this might be through the use of a software time-limiting tool. It's even important to be sure that they are varying what they do online. Encourage them to explore a variety of websites, not just one or two of their favourites.

10 to about 12

During this pre-teen period, many kids want to experience even more independence. If children aren't already doing so, this is a time when they should start using the Internet to help with schoolwork and, perhaps, discover resources for their hobbies, sports activities, and other interests. This is also an age when you have to be concerned not just about what kids see and do on the Internet, but how long they are online. Your job is to help them manage their independence. Set limits on how often and how long kids can be online, and be sure that they are engaged in other activities such as sports, music, and book-reading.

At about age 12 children begin to hone their abstract reasoning skills. With these enhanced skills, they begin to form more of their own values and begin to take on the values of their peers. Before that they're more likely to reflect the values of their parents. It's important at this age to begin to emphasise the concept of credibility. Kids need to understand that not everything they see on the Internet is true or valuable, just as not all advice they get from their peers is valuable. A good way to illustrate this is for them to do a search for sites on subjects they know a lot about – favourite athletes or musicians, subjects they love in school, etc.

12 to about 14

This is the time when many kids become very social and when they are most likely to be interested in online chat. Go over the basic privacy rules with your kids to be sure they understand never to give out information about themselves or to get together with anyone they meet online without first checking with their parents. Also, emphasise the importance of never exchanging photographs with people they don't know. At this age they need to understand clearly the fact that people on the Internet may not be who they appear to be.

This is also an age where many children start expressing interest in sexual matters. It is natural for them to be curious about the opposite (or even same) sex and not unheard of for them to want to look at photos and explore sexual subjects. During this early exploratory period, it is especially important for kids to know that their parents are around and aware of what they are doing. You may not need to be in the same room as your kids the entire time they're on the Net, but they do need to know that you and other family members can walk in and out of the room at any time, and will ask them about what they are doing online.

Don't be alarmed if they are interested in exploring sexual material. How you manage this, of course, depends on your own view of such material. It's important, however, to be aware that some of the materials they might find on the Internet are different – and more explicit – than some of the magazines that may have been around when you were that age. If kids search hard enough, they can probably find websites and newsgroups that explore sexual fantasies that they – and even you – might find disturbing or even frightening. This is probably the strongest argument for Internet filters but it's also an argument for close parental involvement, reinforcing your family's values, and creating a climate of trust and openness between parents and children.

Children at this age are likely to be interested in games that they can download from the Internet to play either online or offline. Some of these games may have content that parents feel is inappropriate, so it's important to be aware of what your kids are doing on the computer, even when they're not connected to the Internet. Monitoring software may help you in this effort.

This is also a period when many parents choose to speak with their children about sexual matters. It may be a good idea to think about how you might react if you discover that your child has visited places on the Internet that you feel are inappropriate.

You can use filtering and monitoring software at this age, but you may start to run into some resistance. What's important is that you are honest with your kids and that they know what you are doing and why you are doing it. If you use filtering software, for example, you need to explain to them that you are doing it to protect them from material that you consider to be harmful. Just as you might not let them go to certain places in your community, you are exercising your parental right to keep them from surfing to certain types of places in cyberspace.

14 to about 17

This can be one of the most exciting and challenging periods of a child's (and parent's) life. Your teen is beginning to mature physically, emotionally, and intellectually and is anxious to experience increasing independence from parents. To some extent that means loosening up on the reins, but by no means does it mean abandoning your parenting role. Teens are complicated in that they demand both independence and guidance at the same time.

Teens are also more likely to engage in risky behaviour both online and offline. While the likelihood of a teen being abducted by someone he meets in a chat room is extremely low, there is always the possibility that he will meet someone online who makes him feel good and makes him want to strike up an in-person relationship. It is extremely important that teens understand that people they meet online are not necessarily who they seem to be.

Although it's sometimes difficult to indoctrinate teens with safety information, they can often understand the need to be on guard against those who might exploit them. Teens need to understand that to be in control of themselves means being vigilant, on the alert for people who might hurt them.

The greatest danger is that a teen will get together offline with someone she meets online. If she does meet someone she wants to get together with, it's important that she not go alone and that she meet that person in a public place.

It's important for parents to remember what it was like when they were teenagers. Set reasonable expectations and don't overreact if and when you find out that your teen has done something online that you don't approve of. That doesn't mean that you shouldn't take it seriously and exercise appropriate control and discipline, but pick your battles and try to look at the bigger picture.

If your teen confides in you about something scary or inappropriate that he encountered online, your first response shouldn't be to take away his Internet privileges. Try to be supportive and work with your teen to help prevent this from happening in the future. And remember that your teen will soon be an adult and needs to know not just how to behave but how to exercise judgement, reaching her own conclusions on how to explore the 'net and life in general in a safe and productive manner.

■ Information from GetNetWise – visit http://kids.getnetwise.org or see page 41 for address details.

© Get Netwise

Illegal images of children go unreported

Memorandum of understanding highlights changes to the Sexual Offences Act 2003

73 per cent of network managers would not report illegal images of children to the police, despite internally disciplining the employee committing the offence, according to research released today (18 October 2004) from the Internet Watch Foundation.

The research of 1000 senior IT professionals at the UK's leading companies also highlighted that 87 per cent of those interviewed were not aware of changes to the UK law and guidelines on handling child abuse content found on their networks.

> **73 per cent of network managers would not report illegal images of children to the police, despite internally disciplining the employee committing the offence**

Despite 68 per cent of respondents believing they understood what constituted a potentially illegal image of a child, only a quarter were able to give the correct age of a 'child' in this context – currently 18, making indecent images of children aged 16 and 17 illegal.

The Memorandum of Understanding between the Association of Chief Police Officers (ACPO) and the Crown Prosecution Service (CPS), announced today, outlines the specific circumstances under which IT professionals could claim a defence under the new legislation.

This defence is intended to reassure people such as staff in Internet Service Providers (ISP) and systems management who may have a role in identifying and securing such data for evidential and investigative purposes, that they can do so without fear of prosecution.

The Sexual Offences Act (SOA) 2003 came into force in May 2004 and reverses the burden of proof for individuals who download potentially illegal child abuse images.

It also introduces a conditional defence to any such allegation to protect IT professionals who may need to 'make', download and save potentially illegal child abuse images, as evidence, in order for the content to be assessed by either a Law Enforcement Agency or other 'relevant' body such as the IWF.

'The results of the survey came as something as a shock, but are indicative of the lack of understanding and fear when it comes to the topic of illegal images,' explained Peter Robbins, Chief Executive Officer at the IWF.

'It is vital that any organisation providing Internet access to employees understands how to deal with these types of images. Company policies must be in line with current UK legislation and internal procedures should be clearly and regularly explained to staff.

'We know that no UK company condones illegal practices, more especially when it means images of child abuse, but we need to educate IT managers as to the correct procedures.'

Any individuals convicted of intentionally downloading paedophilic material for reasons unrelated to the law, can be liable for up to 10 years' imprisonment if prosecuted.

■ Information reprinted with kind permission from the Internet Watch Foundation – visit www.iwf.org.uk or see page 41 for address details.

© IWF

The Virtual Global Taskforce

A new approach to fighting online child abuse at www.virtualglobaltaskforce.com

A new web-based initiative will be launched today (26 January 2005) to deter and prevent individuals from committing child abuse online. The new website has been pioneered by the UK's National Crime Squad in association with UK industry leaders and law enforcement counterparts in Australia, Canada, the US, and Interpol. The Virtual Global Taskforce partnership aims to make the Internet a safer place for children and a more hostile place for paedophiles.

Recent research conducted by ICM revealed that 89% of British adults agreed that there should be a great deal or fair amount of co-operation between the UK police and international law enforcement agencies to help improve child safety online. The Virtual Global Taskforce provides the ideal platform for delivering improved international co-operation.

The website will act as a gateway to information on how to use the Internet safely, and will link to a range of support agencies that can advise and support victims of abuse. It will also facilitate the ability of Internet users to report online child abuse in a secure and confidential environment. The aim is for the website to become a 'one stop shop' for all information about child protection online.

'The Virtual Global Taskforce is an excellent initiative which brings together law enforcement agencies and industry from around the world,' said Home Office Minister, Paul Goggins. 'It is only through building partnerships like these that we can be effective in protecting children and making the Internet safe for children.

'Through the Home Secretary's Task Force on Child Protection on the Internet we have worked with industry, child welfare groups and law enforcement, and we are now providing safer Internet services and advice to children and their parents. Child protection on the Internet is an issue where the UK has consistently led the world in our commitment to tackling the problem, in our readiness to work in partnership with all those who have a role to play, and in our ability to think innovatively about solutions.

'The Virtual Global Taskforce website builds on this work and pulls together safety advice from different countries and, through industry partners, makes this advice easily available to children and parents around the world. The Virtual Global Taskforce and its website are an excellent example of innovative leadership.'

Jim Gamble, Deputy Director General of the UK's National Crime Squad, and Chair of the Virtual Global Taskforce, explained the importance of global working:

'The Virtual Global Taskforce is a unique partnership in the history of law enforcement. Child abuse is one of the worst crimes to affect today's society and we in the UK must break away from thinking that we can tackle this issue within our own borders. Internet-users access a worldwide service and we must tackle abuse from a worldwide perspective. That is why strategic partnerships with partners across the globe are so vital to the success of this initiative. Police across the world must work as one on this.

'And law enforcement can't work alone. A critical factor in the success of the Virtual Global Taskforce is its innovative partnership with industry to help make the Internet safer by design. The founding VGT Industry Partners in the UK – Microsoft/MSN, AOL(UK), Vodafone and BT – are working with the VGT to develop this collaboration. Partners will develop mutual understanding within the international online child protection community and cooperate on the introduction of best practice for protection of children within the industry.

'Our message is simple. Those who use the Internet to search for and share images of child abuse, or to approach children in chat rooms to "groom" them for sexual abuse, must be aware that the Internet is not an anonymous place. The Internet needs to be safe and through this website and other initiatives we are doing all we can to achieve this.'

The Internet Watch Foundation has also been working with the VGT team since its inception and will be featured as a partner organisation on the website.

'We are pleased to be working with national and international Law Enforcement Agencies in this way and welcome this new initiative. It builds on existing strong partnerships between the IWF, industry and police which has led to a successful UK model of co-operation and pro-active work in tackling paedophilic content online.' – Peter Robbins, CEO, IWF.

■ The above information is re-printed with kind permission from the Internet Watch Foundation – visit www.iwf.org.uk for more or see page 41 for contact details.

© IWF

Child abuse, child pornography and the Internet

Executive summary

Modern society has always found it difficult to detect and prevent child sex abuse, the majority of which has taken place within existing family or social circles or in certain institutional settings. The arrival of the Internet has added to this difficulty by opening up new ways for paedophiles to reach and abuse children.

The Internet has also opened up new means of distributing images of the sexual abuse of children. In pre-Internet days police seizures generally yielded only a handful of pictures. Today it is not uncommon for a single suspect to be arrested with tens of thousands of images on his computer. In 2003 one man in Lincolnshire was found with 450,000 child abuse images and a private individual in New York was found with 1,000,000.

The global nature of the Internet brings with it jurisdictional and logistical problems that add yet another layer of complexity. Detection, prevention, the identification and rescue of victims have become even harder. The speed at which the technology has grown, and can change, adds another twist.

Many paedophiles acknowledge that exposure to child abuse images fuels their sexual fantasies and plays an important part in leading them to commit hands-on sexual offences against children. Because the Internet is facilitating larger numbers of individuals becoming involved in collecting and possessing child abuse images, it follows that it is highly likely that more children are therefore now being abused than would otherwise have been the case. Moreover, whereas in the past child abuse images were mainly simply exchanged between collectors, organised crime is now involved, producing large numbers of pictures for sale.

Several studies appear to support the idea that there is a definite link between possessing and collecting child abuse images and being involved in abusing children. The largest study suggests that one in three of those arrested solely for possessing child abuse images is likely to be involved, or to have been involved, in hands-on abuse. Others think that the proportion is much higher and that, in any event, everyone found in possession of child abuse images should be investigated and assessed on that basis.

In the UK the current legal framework in respect of child abuse images was established in 1988. In that year 35 people were proceeded against by the police. In 2001 the number was 549, an increase of 1,500 per cent. In total, between 1988 and the end of 2001, 3,022 people were either cautioned or charged with child pornography offences. The annual rate of increase was running well in excess of 33 per cent when, in 2002, under Operation Ore – arising from a single law enforcement action in the US – the UK police were handed the names of 6,500 people who had used credit cards to buy child abuse images from one website. Over 2,300 of these have now been arrested but they have not yet fed through to the published crime statistics.

The huge increase in arrests arising from Operation Ore is putting enormous pressures on the police, probation and court services and also calls into question whether or not all defendants are being assessed satisfactorily.

The Internet is facilitating a major increase in children and young people being exposed to a wide range of age-inappropriate or illegal sexual and other kinds of material. No one knows what the long-term effects will be of this exposure but parents, teachers and others with a responsibility for children are greatly anxious.

It is clear that parents, teachers and others with responsibility for children must educate their children about the Internet and how to avoid or deal with problems they may encounter on it. Parents and teachers can also be reasonably expected to take steps themselves to supervise and protect children, but it seems equally clear that the Internet in-

dustry in the widest sense must similarly accept a continuing duty to do all they reasonably can at a technological level to ensure children using their services will not come to any avoidable harm. Neither should the industry be indifferent to the possibility that the service they are providing might undermine parental preferences in respect of how they bring up their children. The fact that children at some time or other seek to evade rules laid down by their parents or teachers, is no reason for saying that parents and teachers should therefore abandon the effort and have no rules at all. Rules describe standards.

Within the UK, the government's Internet Task Force on Child Protection has played a decisive leadership role in formulating new laws and developing the child safety agenda. Most of the UK's leading Internet companies have played an active part in the Task Force and have responded positively to its recommendations, but there remains a series of larger reforms that ought to be acted upon. The industry also needs to find new technologically based solutions to assist the police and others in dealing with the new types of Internet misuse that are emerging. Furthermore, with the advent of the new GPRS and 3G mobile phone networks, the Internet is about to go mobile on a large scale, supported by new, sophisticated telephone handsets. Almost all of the issues of child safety on the Internet that exist today become much more complex when the Internet goes on the street.

Given the pre-eminent position of the US in almost anything and everything to do with the Internet, we must look to the US government and law enforcement agencies to increase their effectiveness against the criminals who are using US-based resources to distribute child abuse images across all continents. We must also strengthen international efforts to deal with the rising tide of child abuse images starting to come out of other countries, often in poorer parts of the world.

Whichever way one looks at it the Internet is an enormously important and valuable technological achievement. But that is not to say that civil society has simply to sit back and accept as inevitable whatever is served up to it by the industry.

Finding a solution to the problem of child safety on the Internet is important in its own right, but as long as acceptable solutions evade us, much that is dynamic, valuable and indisputably legitimate about the Internet is also threatened.

■ The above information was written by John Carr, an Internet Consultant for NCH – please visit www.nch.org.uk or see page 41 for contact details.

© NCH

Personal safety tips

Using the Internet

Prepare
- Agree with parents/guardians in advance what sort of sites you will be visiting. Make sure they know before you enter any chat rooms.
- Watch out for websites that have adult/over-18s warnings. These will not be suitable for you – your parents can easily find out if you have visited them!

Avoid risk
- Choose a nickname to use in chat rooms and newsgroups. Never use your real name.
- Never use a nickname that is suggestive e.g. Miss Hot Pants.
- Don't give out personal info e.g. name, address, phone number or school name.
- Try to make it hard for people to guess your real name. For example, it's easy to guess that someone with the nickname 'luap' is really called Paul.
- Passwords are private – make sure they are at least six characters long and keep them secret. If someone knows your password, they can use your account and their Internet use will be charged to your parents' phone bill.
- Internet providers will never ask you for your password except when you first sign on.
- Remember that people you meet on the Internet might not be who they say they are. Some adults may pretend to be children and try to persuade you to meet with them.
- If you want to meet people you have talked to over the Internet make sure you let your parents/guardians know first. Arrange to meet in a busy, public place and get an adult to go with you – they can always go away again once you are sure the person is who they say they are.
- Beware! Viruses can be spread through email attachments. Only open emails from people you know. If you are uncertain, then delete the email.

What if?
- You think someone knows your password – change it straight away.
- You get an email saying that computer problems mean the company has to ask you to confirm your password – delete it from your mailbox without answering.
- Someone is making offensive comments or using threatening language in a chat room or newsgroup – leave the chat room immediately and report that person to the person in charge of monitoring the chat room.
- Never assume it won't happen to you!

■ The above information is from the Milly's Fund website which can be found at www.millysfund.org.uk, or see page 41 for address details.

© Milly's Fund

New centre to protect children online

Information from the Home Office

As part of 'Connecting the UK: the digital strategy' to be outlined by the Prime Minister, the Home Office today (1 April 2005) announced that the Government is to set up a new Centre for Child Protection on the Internet to support the police and child protection agencies. The Centre will target paedophiles using the Internet to distribute illegal images and 'groom' children.

The Centre's aim will be to reduce the harm caused to children, families and societies by child abuse facilitated through the Internet.

The Centre is supported by the members of the Home Secretary's Internet Task Force, including the Association of Chief Police Officers (ACPO), the Internet Watch Foundation, children's charities and the Internet industry. The Centre will be attached to the Serious Organised Crime Agency (SOCA) and will be operational by April 2006. It will be staffed by specialist police officers as well as child protection and Internet industry experts, and will be a focal point for the online element of child protection work.

The new Centre will:

- provide a single 24/7 point of contact for the public, law enforcers, industry, and other organisations for reporting targeting of children online;
- offer information and advice to victims and potential victims of abuse and parents;
- assess and disseminate international and domestic intelligence on online and offline offenders, including paedophiles and other serious sex offenders;
- crime prevention and crime reduction strategies to reduce the harm caused by online child abuse;
- undertake proactive investigations to identify high priority targets;
- manage the national database of child abuse images ('Childbase') and implement links to other systems; and
- provide specialist guidance and good practice to local agencies.

Home Secretary Charles Clarke said: 'Protecting children is a key priority for the Government, and that applies online as well as offline.

Online abuse by definition crosses geographical police force boundaries – so it makes much more sense to tackle the problem at national level.

'The new centre I am announcing today will protect children online, help the police do their job more effectively, and catch and prosecute child abusers who target children through the Internet. Parents know how to protect their children from danger offline; we want to help protect their children online in the same way.

'The Task Force we set up in 2001 to tackle this problem has shown that our law enforcers, the Internet industry and our children's charities are all committed to helping us stamp out online child abuse, and today's announcement is the next step towards closer co-operation.'

Stuart Hyde, ACPO lead on Child Abuse on the Internet and Assistant Chief Constable of West Midlands Police, said: 'We have worked with our partners in government, industry and the voluntary sector to create the business case for the National Centre. I am delighted that we are now seeing the fruits of that labour. As part of SOCA the Centre will enable the UK to have the best response to combating child abuse online.

'The National Centre will be a major contribution to making the Internet safer. I would like to thank my colleagues and partners for their support in turning this idea into a reality.'

Trevor Pearce, Director General of the National Crime Squad, said: 'We are delighted with the announcement today of the creation of the new Centre and look forward to working closely with Ministers to deliver this by April 2006.

'UK law enforcement has been at the forefront of tackling online child abuse and it is in recognition of our

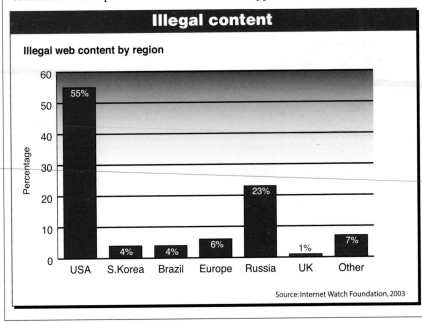

Illegal content

Illegal web content by region

USA 55%, S.Korea 4%, Brazil 4%, Europe 6%, Russia 23%, UK 1%, Other 7%

Source: Internet Watch Foundation, 2003

achievements that we can now create a world first. Working with child welfare agencies and industry partners, the new Centre will allow us to build on existing foundations and deliver a step-change in child protection.'

NSPCC director of services for children and young people Wes Cuell said: 'The Internet Safety Centre is the result of months of partnership working between the NSPCC and the police. We are delighted to see the foundations we helped to build come to fruition as the Centre marks a big step towards making the Internet a safer place for children and young people.

'The growth of Internet use has led to an explosion in the distribution of child pornography, and with the advent of new technology, children are at greater risk than ever before. Placing the new Centre within SOCA puts online child abuse as a national police priority for the first time and sends out a strong message that the Internet is no longer a marketplace for abusive images of children'.

John Carr of NCH, the children's charity, and a member of the Government's Internet Task Force, said: 'This National Centre marks a big step forward in tackling online child abuse. It's the first example anywhere in the world of the police, the industry, child welfare bodies and the Government working together under one roof to tackle Internet child abuse.'

Mike Galvin, BT's director of Internet Operations, said: 'BT welcomes the news that the Government will support a dedicated centre for Internet Safety in the UK. The centre will make it easier for all of us in the Internet industry to report abuse, especially child abuse. We fully support the work of the Centre to facilitate faster victim identification and assistance as well as faster abuser profiling and arrests.

'This announcement further demonstrates the Government's and the industry's commitment to seek to make the UK the safest place in the world for children to use the Internet, which is the main aim of the Internet Taskforce.'

■ The above information is from the Home Office: www.homeoffice.gov.uk

Internet pornography offences quadrupled in two years

Information from NCH

Arrests and convictions for Internet pornography offences against children have quadrupled in just two years, leading children's charity NCH reveals.

New figures show that the number of people cautioned or charged with child pornography offences in 2003 was 2,234, up from only 549 in 2001.

This is also a huge increase of 6,500 per cent since 1988 – when the current legal framework for child pornography offences was established and only 35 cases were recorded.

NCH argues these latest figures highlight the urgent need for funding for a new national centre to combat online offences against children.

NCH Internet safety advisor John Carr says: 'These new and astonishing numbers reflect the arrests made during Operation Ore. But given ongoing police activity, the worry is

that they represent not a blip but a new "normality". Many police admit that they are still only touching the tip of a very ugly iceberg.

'There is now widespread agreement about the need for a new, high powered national centre to tackle Internet crimes against children. The only thing there is not yet an agreement about is who should pay for it. We hope ministers can resolve this very soon. What NCH says is that we want a new national centre – and we want it now.'

These latest shocking statistics also highlight the importance of Internet Service Providers (ISPs) following the lead, provided by BT and Vodafone, in blocking access to known child pornography websites.

NCH will be asking the Home Secretary to investigate how many ISPs in the UK have yet to block access to these known illegal sites, using the Cleanfeed system which BT pioneered.

Mr Carr adds: 'Child pornography on the Internet is a modern curse and ISPs have a critical part to play in stamping it out. BT and Vodafone showed the way. We want everyone else to follow or, I am afraid, legislation compelling them to do so will be inevitable.'

■ Information from NCH – see page 41 for address details.

Spam

Information from CyberAngels

What is spam?

While the legal definition may vary from state to state, country to country and even person to person, spam is junk or unsolicited email. Junk email, or spam, comes in a couple of different 'flavours' including unsolicited bulk email (UBE spam) and unsolicited commercial email (UCE spam) although the concept behind the two terms are essentially the same – that is sending email to multiple recipients who have not requested it nor consented to having their email address(es) included on such a mailing list.

Often, spam is used to advertise (or spamvertise) services or goods of dubious, or even illegal, nature

---

Often, spam is used to advertise (or spamvertise) services or goods of dubious, or even illegal, nature such as make money fast (MMF) schemes, multi-level marketing (MLM) or pyramid schemes, pornography, etc.

How do spammers get email addresses?

Spammers use a variety of methods to obtain email addresses but one of the most popular is to use a spambot or spider. Spambots or spiders are specialised programs that search websites, forums or newsgroups for email addresses. Probably the easiest finds are via personal websites where owners list their email addresses by creating hyperlinks so people can easily email them or put up guestbooks that show the email addresses of those who post to them.

Scanning people's AIM/AOL, ICQ, mIRC and other profiles is another good source of information and addresses for spammers. Many people think nothing of posting not only their email address but other personal data such as their real name or telephone number to such profiles.

Often, spammers receive email addresses directly from the future recipients of their junk. When filling out forms on various websites people usually use their real email address. Unless the site is very well known and you are familiar with their privacy policy you are playing a game of roulette any time you post your personal email address to the web. Also make sure when you complete a form on a website that you are not requesting further contact via a selected or checked 'Send Info' box.

And lastly, spammers sell lists of email addresses to one another. So once your address becomes 'known' to one spammer the problem can quickly escalate beyond your wildest imaginings.

Preventing spam

There are quite a few things you can do to prevent or reduce your personal email address from being spidered or collected.

If you post messages to bulletin boards or forums either don't publicly post your email address or use a throwaway address. A throwaway address is just what it sounds like – an address that you use for a while then discard. Such addresses are usually free web-based accounts via websites such as bigfoot.com, hotmail.com, yahoo.com, etc. If your regular email address is, for example, unclejohn53@aol.com don't go out and set up an address such as unclejohn53@bigfoot.com for a throwaway account. Doing so makes it far too easy to determine your real email address. And don't get too 'attached' to such throwaway addresses – the intention is to use them until you begin receiving spam and then get a new one.

Posting to newsgroups can be done via the web or via your ISP using a newsreader such as Outlook Express or other software. If you will be posting to newsgroups via the web use a throwaway email address as indicated above.

If you will be posting to newsgroups via a newsreader another

09:05 am, Sally checks her email.

option available is to edit your newsreader configuration so that our email address is incorrect. Instead of your Reply-To address being your regular email address, set it up to point to your throwaway address. Or you can 'munge' your Reply-To address so that instead of showing your real address as 123@abc.net it shows it as 123@nospam.abc.net or even 123@spammerssuck.abc.net.

About signatures – either remove your real email address from your signatures or munge them in such a way that spambots or spiders won't readily detect them as valid addresses. For instance, instead of your signature file containing your address in the usual format, edit it to look something like 123(at)abc.net or even 123(at)abc(dot)net. Doing so means a little more work for someone who wants to send you an email but it also means that a spider or spambot won't detect it as a valid address.

If you have a webpage or website, don't post your real email address anywhere on it. Some alternatives are to munge the address as shown above, post a throwaway address, use a bit of javascript magic to 'hide' your address, or use a form. Of these methods the javascript or the form are the most difficult to implement but they also provide you with the most security.

How can I stop the spam once it starts?

Prevention really is the best cure but the first thing to do is to ensure that what you are receiving really is spam.

Often our children or spouses will subscribe to a mailing list without telling us or we will complete a web form and forget to uncheck the 'Send Info' box. Most forms have one or more of these boxes selected by default. In such cases you are not being spammed but merely receiving mail that you have requested – however unknowingly – and you can safely follow the instructions provided to unsubscribe yourself from the list. Occasionally you may receive emails from someone you only met once or corresponded with briefly and have since forgotten. Again, these do not generally constitute spam.

Some things to look for in determining if you have received spam:

- Multiple 'Received:' lines in the message header
- Promotes a webpage on another site
- Directs replies to an email address in another domain or on another system.

Now that you're certain you have received unsolicited bulk or commercial email (spam) the first thing is NOT to reply to the message or use any 'removal' addresses contained in the message. Replying to such messages or using their removal addresses is usually an exercise in futility because even if the removal address is a valid, live address (often it isn't) you are simply verifying your address is a valid one and almost ensuring that you will be spammed again. Also, do not make the mistake of assuming that any email addresses contained in such emails, especially the reply address, is a valid one.

If you're not unduly offended by the messages you can simply delete them manually or create an inbound filter that will automatically delete them. Outlook, Outlook Express, Eudora and most other current email client software can be configured to perform filtering on incoming emails based on whatever criteria you provide. There are also many add-on utilities for a variety of email softwares that will perform the same function.

You will need to familiarise yourself with your email software to learn how to configure filters or rules. To learn more, try using the Help command and reading the online manual or help files for your particular software and/ or visit the support website.

Filtering spam is not difficult but you will need to keep an eye on things and browse your deleted items folder in your email software periodically to ensure that valid emails are not being deleted. Much better is to simply create a JunkMail directory and have filtered email placed there instead of automatically deleting it.

You can filter email by the sender's address (these change often), the subject line (these too change) or a number of other criteria. Be careful not to implement a filter on an entire domain (such as *.cn, *.com, *.net, etc.) because doing so could prevent you from receiving desired email.

One of the best allies in the fight against spam is your own ISP. Each one has its own policies and services but most provide support and resources to assist you. If your ISP has a search command on their website try searching for the word spam to see what information is available. If there is no search command on their website or you can't find any mention of the word spam, email or call them and ask!

I can't tell you how many times we've received emails from desperate people who are being relentlessly spammed only to go to their ISP's website and locate all of the spam info for them and refer them back to their own ISP for assistance. In most cases, your own ISP should be your first contact and will be the best source of information in terms of what options are open to you and how to properly report occurrences of spam to them to maximise their ability to put a stop to it.

Many ISPs have the ability to filter spam at the server level before you ever see it. Ask your ISP if they provide this service, if it's free or costs extra, and/or if it is user configureable. Fighting back by tracing where the spam originates and complaining to their ISP is a viable option for some people but is beyond the current scope of this document.

Phishing

Information from BankSafeOnline

What is phishing?

Phishing is the name given to the practice of sending emails at random purporting to come from a genuine company operating on the Internet, in an attempt to trick customers of that company into disclosing information at a bogus website operated by fraudsters. These emails usually claim that it is necessary to 'update' or 'verify' your customer account information and they urge people to click on a link from the email which takes them to the bogus website. Any information entered on the bogus website will be captured by the criminals for their own fraudulent purposes.

How can I prevent myself being a victim of phishing?

The key thing to remember is that you should remain alert and be suspicious of all unsolicited or unexpected emails you receive, even if they appear to originate from a trusted source. Although your bank may contact you by email, they will never ask you to reconfirm your login or security password information by clicking on a link in an email and visiting a web site. Stop to think about how your bank normally communicates with you and never disclose your password or personal information to any site which asks you for it by email.

Banks will never contact you by email to ask you to enter your password or any other sensitive information by clicking on a link and visiting a web site.

The emails are sent out completely at random in the hope of reaching a live email address of a customer with an account at the bank being targeted.

How to spot a phishing email

1. Who is the email from?

Phishing emails can look like they come from a real bank email address. Unfortunately the way Internet email works makes it a relatively simple matter for phishers to create a fake entry in the 'From:' box.

The email address that appears in the 'From' field of an email is NOT a guarantee that it came from the person or organisation that it says it did. These emails were not sent using the bank's own systems.

2. Who is the email for?

The emails are sent out at random to bulk email lists and the fraudsters will almost certainly not know your real name or indeed anything else about you, and will address you in vague terms like 'Dear Valued Customer'.

3. Take a closer look at the email – does it look 'phishy'?!

The first thing to remember is that banks will never write to you and ask you for your password or any other sensitive information by email. The message is also likely to contain odd 'spe11ings' or cApitALs in the 'Subject:' box (this is an attempt to get around spam filter software), as well as grammatical and spelling errors.

Never log-on to your online banking account by clicking on a link in an email. Open your web browser and type the bank's address in yourself.

If in any doubt about the validity of an email purporting to come from your bank, contact them on an advertised phone number.

4. Where's that hyperlink going to?

Unfortunately it is all too possible to disguise a link's real destination, so the displayed link and anything which shows up in the status bar of your email programme can easily be falsified.

How to spot a phishing web site

What's the site address?

There are many ways of disguising the true location of a fake web site in the address bar, if you visit a web site after clicking on a link from an email. The site address may start with the genuine site's domain name, but that is no guarantee that it points to the real site. Other tricks include using numerical addresses, registering a similar web address (such as www.mybank-verify.com), or even inserting a false address bar into the browser window. Many of the links from these pages may actually go to the genuine web site, but don't be fooled.

Beware of fraudulent pop-up windows

Instead of displaying a completely fake web site, the fraudsters may load the genuine web site in the main browser window and then place their own fake pop-up window over the top of it. Displayed like this, you can see the address bar of the real web site in the background, although any information you type into the pop-up window will be collected by the fraudsters for their own usage.

To access your online banking account, type the address into a new window yourself. The address of your genuine bank site will start

https and will include a small padlock in the bottom of the browser window.

Reporting suspicious emails

If you do receive a suspicious email, please inform your bank as directed on their web site and forward the email reports@banksafeonline.org.uk

Remember:

- Banks will never email you to request that you 'confirm' or 'update' your password or any personal information by clicking on a link and visiting a web site
- Treat all unsolicited emails with

caution and never click on links from such emails and enter any personal information
- To log-on to Internet banking, open your web browser and type the address in yourself
- If in doubt about the validity of an email, or if you think that you may have disclosed information to a fraudulent site, contact your bank immediately on an advertised number.

- The above information is from the BankSafeOnline website – visit www.banksafeonline.org.uk

© *BankSafeOnline*

Pharming out-scams phishing

Information from Wired

By Michelle Delio

First came phishing scams, in which con artists hooked unwary Internet users one by one into compromising their personal data. Now the latest cyber-swindle, pharming, threatens to reel in entire schools of victims.

The rise in Internet banking, online shopping and electronic bill paying has created a wide potential profit zone for criminals

Pharmers simply redirect as many users as possible from the legitimate commercial websites they'd intended to visit and lead them to malicious ones. The bogus sites, to which victims are redirected without their knowledge or consent, will likely look the same as a genuine site. But when users enter their login name and password, the information is captured by criminals.

'Phishing is to pharming what a guy with a rod and a reel is to a Russian trawler. Phishers have to

approach their targets one by one. Pharmers can scoop up many victims in a single pass,' said Chris Risley, president and chief executive officer of Nominum, a provider of IP address infrastructure technology for businesses.

Emailed viruses that rewrite local host files on individual PCs, like the Banker Trojan, have been used to conduct smaller-scale pharming attacks. Host files convert standard URLs into the numeric strings a computer understands. A computer with a compromised host file will go to the wrong website even if a user types in the correct URL.

The most alarming pharming threat is DNS poisoning, which can cause a large group of users to be herded to bogus sites. DNS – the domain name system – translates web and email addresses into numerical strings, acting as a sort of telephone directory for the Internet. If a DNS directory is 'poisoned' – altered to contain false information regarding

which web address is associated with what numeric string – users can be silently shuttled to a bogus website even if they type in the correct URL.

'DNS poisoning has been around for over a decade now,' said Gregg Mastoras, senior security analyst at Sophos. 'Many would argue that the DNS system we all depend so heavily on has inherent design vulnerabilities, and because of the initial design flaws there have been a variety of methods used to create successful attacks.

'So while DNS poisoning is not new, the dramatic rise of phishing, and more importantly the complexity of the new pharming attacks, is cause for some concern,' Mastoras said.

Phishing is essentially an old con game updated to take advantage of new technology. Similarly, although DNS attack tactics used by pharmers have been around for a while, the rise in Internet banking, online shopping and electronic bill paying has created a wide potential profit zone for criminals eager to snag login information and credit card and bank account numbers.

According to information provided by the SANS Internet Storm Center and Internet-monitoring firm Netcraft, this past weekend (12-13 March 2005) would-be pharmers attempted to exploit a known vulnerability in Symantec's firewall, redirecting some users from eBay, Google and weather.com to three sites that attempted to install spyware on visitors' computers.

Security experts believe the attack was just a trial run; it was limited in scope and few users seem to have been affected.

However, Mastoras says other sophisticated attacks that take advantage of the flaws in DNS protocols are also currently being tested.

In one example, Mastoras said, Barclays Bank was recently targeted. The phishers sent messages that included a link whose first letters were the correct 'barclays.co.uk' but then had additional letters that misdirected the user.

Mastoras called this particular method DNS wildcards. A wildcard DNS record is used to manage mistyped email addresses, but has lately been used by spammers and now by phishers, he said.

'DNS just isn't as secure as we'd like to think it is,' said Nominum's Risley. 'Every Internet request has to go through a DNS server, and

Plenty of computer-savvy criminals lurking on the Internet are eager and able to conduct sophisticated large-scale crimes

malicious hackers realised a long time ago the profit potential in hacking DNS records.'

Nominum's chief scientist, Paul Mockapetris, helped to pioneer the Internet domain name system through the Internet Engineering Task Force in 1983. Mockapetris also designed the DNS architecture that is still in use today, wrote the specifications and coded the first implementation.

Risley said Mockapetris firmly believes it's time to refresh DNS, and that Mockapetris never expected DNS and BIND – the most widely used DNS software package for Unix/Linux machines – to be used on today's huge public systems. Nominum now sells commercial alternatives to open-source BIND and other DNS solutions.

Still, some security experts believe pharmers will not widely deploy DNS-poisoning techniques.

'Could DNS poisoning be an issue? Yes. Will it be a major issue? Probably not,' said Mikko H. Hypponen,

director of antivirus research at security services vendor F-Secure. Hypponen cited the skill level needed to hack a high-level DNS server as a major deterrent.

Others say plenty of computer-savvy criminals lurking on the Internet are eager and able to conduct sophisticated large-scale crimes.

'I believe that DNS-poisoning pharmers will become more of a threat this year, as there is money to be made on a large scale here,' said Patrick Hinojosa, chief technical officer at Panda Software, a security technology provider.

'If the right domain can be hijacked or the right DNS record poisoned, a group could make off with data that could be used to accomplish huge financial rip-offs. The problem is that the end user sitting at his computer thinks he's at the correct site because he typed the right URL into the browser,' Hinojosa said.

Experts say pharming could be combated if browsers would authenticate websites' identities. Web browser toolbars like one offered by Netcraft can alert users by displaying the true physical location of a website's host. US customers, for example, would likely pause before typing in their passwords when a website that looks like their local bank's site is reported to be hosted in Russia.

'What would go a long way to protecting people would be server-side certificates,' said Hinojosa. 'But any certificate system would have to be widespread to be effective.'

Some financial institutions, whose users are the prime targets of phishing and pharming scams, are experimenting with 'multi-factor authentication' logins, including things like single-use passwords and automatic telephone call-backs confirming that a transaction is about to take place. Such practices can limit the havoc a malicious hacker can wreak with a collection of stolen logins and passwords.

■ The above information is from the Wired website which can be found at www.wired.com

Chat and instant messaging

Information from CyberAngels

Safety tips

Nicks and profiles

Avoid choosing provocative or identifiable nicknames (such as sexygal or fran_in_philly). Keep personal information out of your online profile.

Receiving files

If you are accepting files from someone you aren't that well acquainted with, or even a friend, viruses can be passed. Be sure to scan all files with an up-to-date virus scanner before opening.

Minors

All minors should be supervised by an adult while using chat or IM programs. Teach your child to not talk to strangers – lurking in chat rooms is a favourite way for paedophiles to meet children.

Harassment

If you (or anyone else) are a recipient of harassment it is best to record the offender. Try notifying the server (e.g. AOL) or saving chat room to a file...

Etiquette

Good etiquette should be used on the Internet as in person. People chatting should refrain from making any comments they would not use in 'everyday life'.

Chat programs

'Chatting' on the Internet has become a popular way for people to talk (chat) in a group (room) who share similar interests and/or age groups. 'Chatting' is considered the same as talking, only you are typing words rather than having an actual 'real' verbal communication. More often, there are more than one 'conversation'/statement (s) going on simultaneously in a given time/room. This is why they are called 'chat rooms'; however, keep in mind not all chat rooms are monitored.

Instant messaging

It seems we get faster and faster each day; never satisfied with the latest technology. Thus, email is too slow. People are turning by the thousands to instant message programs. What is an instant message program? An instant message program is a program that allows two or more people to talk without waiting for email (or in real time). There is usually a box of some kind, a split screen, or some sort of small screen where the messages are passed back and forth. Some of these programs allow you to see what the person is writing as they are writing it. They are usually free, easy to download, and fairly simple to operate. Several of the programs allow you to leave a message so that when the recipient signs on, they see the message you left. Others will tell you that the recipient is not available, thus, no message can be left at that time.

The instant message program is good for private conversations with friends and family. It is in real time, it's easy, and it's quick. It allows the sender and recipient to communicate faster than email and cheaper than by telephone. When there are more than two people involved in the message, most programs allow you to add someone to the conversation, similar to a conference call. You can also time stamp some programs by including time and date of conversation. The conversations can then be saved to your hard drive if needed.

There are many things you can do with the message program besides just chat. It can be used to transfer files to another individual and, of course, send photos. The good thing is you can run the program and still access your email or surf the Internet. If you are having a discussion about something in particular, i.e. song lyrics, you can surf the web, obtain the lyrics and send to your recipient without shutting down and restarting your program. Most instant message programs allow you to chose your font, colours and, in some cases, background. You can customise it to suit your needs or personality.

■ Information from CyberAngels – visit www.cyberangels.org or see page 41 for address details.

© CyberAngels

Dealing with computer and Internet addiction

Information from AskMen.com

Does your wife, girlfriend, parent, or sibling ever tell you that you are spending too much time on the computer? That you are neglecting your responsibilities? That you are becoming more irritable and unsociable? Have you ever stayed up until 3a.m. surfing the web? Downloading music, backgrounds or porn? Well, if you've answered 'yes' to at least one of these questions, then you might discover that you are, indeed, addicted to your screen and cyberspace.

Computer/Internet addiction was never an issue in the 1980s. That's because the Internet was not yet popular with the general public. Big companies and defence organisations were the first ones to ever start implementing the technology into their systems in the early 80s, and then a huge market was discovered for this technology to get big… very big.

In the early 90s, psychiatrists and clinicians were beginning to hear of a new medical term, 'Internet addiction'. At first, this was met with a lot of scepticism and denial; however, it became evident that the more people logged on to cyberspace, the more they got hooked.

The 10 symptoms you need to watch out for

According to Dr James Fearing of the National Counselling Centre in Minneapolis, these are the basic 10 symptoms individuals need to look out for:

1. **No Limitations:** A demonstrated 'loss of control' when trying to stop or limit the amount of time on the computer. (Breaking promises to self or others. Promising to quit or cut down and not being able to do so.)

2. **Lying:** Being dishonest or minimising the extent of the time you stay on the computer, or covering up or being dishonest about what activities you participate in when on the computer.

3. **Harmful Results:** Negative consequences experienced by the computer user or his/her friends or family as a direct result of time or activities spent on the computer.

4. **Improper Behaviour:** Participation in high risk or normally unacceptable behaviours when using the computer. Compromising your morals and values based on the opportunity to remain anonymous and protected on the computer (a good test for this is to ask yourself if your spouse, partner or family would approve of what you were doing on the computer).

5. **Misplaced Priorities:** An over-developed sense of importance for the computer in one's life. Defending your right to use the computer as much as desired, regardless of the fact that people in your life are feeling left out and neglected (denial of the problem and justification; not being able to hear or feel what the other people are saying regarding your computer behaviour).

6. **Rapture:** Mixed feelings of euphoria (a 'rush'), combined with feelings of guilt brought on by either the inordinate amount of time spent on the computer or the abnormal behaviour acted out while using the computer.

7. **Despair:** A feeling of depression or anxiety when something or someone shortens your time or interrupts your plans to use the computer.

8. **Fixation:** Preoccupation with the computer and related activities when you are not using the computer (thinking about the computer and its activities when doing something else; i.e. having a family dinner, working on a project, etc.).

9. **Escapism:** Finding yourself using the computer at times when you are feeling uncomfortable, irritated or sad about something happening in your life (i.e. if you are feeling uncomfortable in your relationship, you will self-medicate and 'hide out' on the computer). Using time on the computer to become externally focused outside yourself as a way to evade what's happening in your life, and avoid feeling the appropriate emotions inside yourself. (Self-medicating.)

10. **Excessive Spending:** Experiencing financial concerns or problems in your life as a result of money being spent on computer hardware, computer online charges, or any other costs associated with computers. (Spending money on computer related items that should have been allocated to other normal living expenses.)

If you recognise at least one of these symptoms, you may have a problem with computer addiction. If you recognise more than two, you are demonstrating a pattern of behaviour that would suggest that you are addicted to your computer and/or the activities on it.

Consequences of addiction

Physical risk factors involved with an addiction to the Internet are comparatively minimal yet notable. While time is not a direct function in defining Internet addiction, generally, addicted users are likely to use the Internet anywhere from forty to eighty hours per week (it becomes like a full-time job), with single sessions that could last up to twenty hours.

To accommodate such excessive use, sleep patterns are typically disrupted due to late-night log-ins. The patient typically stays up past normal bedtime hours and may report staying online until 2, 3, or 4a.m., with the reality of having to wake up for work or school at 6a.m.

In extreme cases, caffeine pills are used to facilitate longer Internet sessions. Such sleep depravation causes excessive fatigue, often making academic or occupational functioning impaired, and may decrease one's immune system, leaving the patient vulnerable to disease.

Additionally, the sedentary act of prolonged computer use may result in a lack of proper exercise and lead to an increased risk for carpal tunnel syndrome, back strain, or eyestrain. While the physical side effects of utilising the Internet are mild compared to chemical dependency, addictive use of the Internet will result in similar familial, academic, and occupational impairment.

Family problems

Marriages, dating relationships, parent-child relationships, and close friendships have been noted to be seriously disrupted by 'net binges'. Patients will gradually spend less time with people in their lives in exchange for solitary time in front of a computer.

Marriages appear to be the most affected as Internet use interferes with responsibilities and obligations at home, and it is typically the spouse who takes on these neglected chores and often feels like a 'Cyberwidow'.

How to overcome the addiction

■ **Practise the opposite**
For example, let's say that your Internet habit involves checking your email first thing in the morning. Instead, you should take a shower or start breakfast first instead of logging on. Or, perhaps you only use the Internet at night, and have an established pattern of coming home and sitting in front of the computer for the remainder of the evening. Then I suggest you wait until after dinner and the news before logging on. Got it?

■ **Set goals**
In order to avoid Internet usage, you should programme structured sessions by setting reasonable goals, perhaps 20 hours instead of the current 40 on the Net.

■ **Develop your inventory**
Start asking yourself, 'What am I missing out on when I spend so much time on the 'net?' Then, write these activities down. You'll be surprised to find out that the list is endless.

■ **Join a support group**
By talking with others who are in the same boat as you, you will (first) make new, real friends, and then you will begin to realise that you are not alone in your fight to overcome this addiction. Support is very important.

■ **Family support**
Seek the support of family members, since they know you better than most people.

Addicted online users tend to use the Internet as an excuse to avoid needed but reluctantly performed daily chores such as doing the laundry, cutting the lawn, or going grocery shopping. Those mundane tasks are ignored as well as important activities such as caring for children. For example, one mother forgot such things as picking up her children after school, making them dinner, and putting them to bed because she became so absorbed in her Internet use.

Similar to alcoholics who will try to hide their addiction, Internet addicts engage in the same lying about how long their Internet sessions really last or hiding bills related to fees for Internet service. These same characteristics create distrust and will hurt the quality of once stable relationships over time.

Academic problems

Although the merits of the Internet make it an ideal research tool, students surf irrelevant websites, engage in chat room gossip, converse with Internet pen pals, and play interactive games at the cost of productive activity.

Alfred University's Provost W. Richard Ott investigated why normally successful students with 1200 to 1300 SAT scores had recently been dismissed. To his surprise, his investigation found that 43% of these students failed school due to extensive patterns of late-night log-ons to the university computer system.

Occupational problems

Internet misuse by employees is a serious concern among managers. The benefits of the Internet such as assisting employees with anything from market research to business communication outweigh the negatives for any company, yet there is a definite concern that it is a distraction to many employees. Any misuse of time in the workplace creates a problem for managers, especially as corporations are providing employees with a tool that can easily be misused.

■ The above information was written by Vatche Bartekian, Stress Management Specialist, and was taken from the AskMen website – visit www.askmen.com for more information.

© AskMen

Hollywood heads to court over movie-swapping

Information from ZDNet

The film industry is set to follow in the litigious path laid by music companies and take on illegal file-swapping in the courts.

Hollywood studios are about to take the long-anticipated step of firing a barrage of lawsuits at some of the most prolific Internet pirates, echoing the legal strategy that the recording industry already has used with limited success.

The civil lawsuits, which will be filed against individual movie file-swappers starting 16 November 2004, represent a kind of legal escalation for an industry that fears its films eventually may be shared on the Internet as widely as songs are today.

'Illegal movie trafficking represents the greatest threat to the economic basis of moviemaking in its 110-year history,' Dan Glickman, president of the Motion Picture Association of America, said in a statement released on Thursday (4 November 2004) after a press conference in Los Angeles.

In a follow-up telephone interview, Glickman said he was not prepared to divulge which file-swapping networks would be targeted in the first round of lawsuits.

www.zdnet.co.uk

Literature the MPAA distributed lists Kazaa, eDonkey and Gnutella as examples of networks where 'illegal digital copies of our member companies' motion pictures' are being traded.

Glickman also would not say whether movie downloaders would be sued, or only those people who make movies available in their shared folders. 'We are targeting folks who illegally traffic in these materials,' he said. 'I'm not going to be more specific.'

Until now, the MPAA's member companies were content with a campaign that pressured universities to curb peer-to-peer piracy, sought new laws from Congress, targeted operators of peer-to-peer networks with civil lawsuits, and tried to convince members of the public to visit the RespectCopyrights.org website.

But the MPAA's initial legal strategy ran aground in August when a federal appeals court ruled that peer-to-peer network operators such as Grokster and StreamCast Networks – which runs Morpheus – could not be held liable for what individual users do. That landmark decision, coupled with the rapid adoption of broadband connections, appears to have prompted the MPAA to target individual users.

MPAA lawyers will rely on the legal playbook invented by the Recording Industry Association of America in its controversial campaign against music pirates. First, the lawyers will record the Internet Protocol addresses of a handful of the most flagrant copyright infringers inhabiting peer-to-peer networks and file what are known as 'John Doe' lawsuits, which list a defendant to be named at a later time. Once the civil suits are filed, the lawyers can ask a federal court to order an Internet service provider to unmask the defendant.

Even more than with the recording industry, though, big bucks are at stake in movie piracy. The MPAA estimates that the average

cost of making, marketing and distributing a movie is about $143m, and the average number of movies swapped on peer-to-peer networks in the United States each day is between 115,000 and 148,000.

California Governor Arnold Schwarzenegger, a Republican, applauded the movie studios' litigation strategy. 'Over 500,000 people are employed by the entertainment industry in California, and it contributes over $30bn annually to our economy,' he said. 'We cannot let illegal movie piracy continue or it will cripple this important industry and seriously hurt California's economy.'

But Public Knowledge, an advocacy group based in Washington, DC, predicted that litigation would not curb movie piracy: 'Simply bringing lawsuits against individual infringers will not solve the problem of infringing activity over P2P networks. First and foremost, it is crucial that the motion picture industry develop new business models that treat the low cost, ubiquity and speed of the Internet as an opportunity, not a threat.'

Peer-to-peer network watchers have said that trading movies has risen sharply in recent months, as broadband has become more common and file-swapping technologies designed to handle large files efficiently have spread. While movie files tend to be roughly 1,000 times the size of individual song files in MP3 format, higher-speed connections, fatter hard drives and cheaper DVD burners are making it easier to download films online.

Illegal movie trafficking represents the greatest threat to the economic basis of moviemaking in its 110-year history

---

A recent survey from network monitoring firm CacheLogic found that BitTorrent, a file-swapping technology used largely to distribute movies, software and TV shows, accounted for more than half of all peer-to-peer network traffic worldwide. CacheLogic, a British analysis firm, estimated that BitTorrent traffic consumes 35 per cent of all Internet traffic.

BayTSP, a company that monitors peer-to-peer networks for movie studios and record labels, said that it sees tens of thousands of separate copies of movies online every month. The most popular movie in October 2004 was *The Terminal*, with about 40,000 copies spread around file-swapping networks, the company said on Thursday.

MPAA's member companies are Buena Vista Pictures Distribution, Sony Pictures Entertainment, Metro-Goldwyn-Mayer Studios, Paramount Pictures, Twentieth Century Fox, Universal City Studios and Warner Bros. Entertainment.

■ Written by Declan McCullagh – to view this article, please go to http://news.zdnet.co.uk/business/legal/0,39020651,39172740,00.htm. ZDNET is a registered service mark of CNET Networks, Inc. ZDNET Logo is a service mark of CNET NETWORKS, Inc.

File sharing

Information from CyberAngels

Vocabulary

Filesharing
Individuals storing files on their hard disk and sharing them with other people either through a P2P network or by uploading them to another server and sharing the address of those files.

Peer-to-peer networks (aka P2P)
Using software that causes your machine to became a mini server, connected to thousands (potentially millions) of other servers – to facilitate the sharing of files from one machine directly to another.

MP3
A popular format online for music files – many software programs exist that allow you to 'squeeze' a song track down to a smaller file that can be saved on your hard disk.

File sharing

Advantages
File-sharing networks have become wildly popular, they allow individuals to download games, applications, music and movies and more virtually for free. They are simple to use, and allow people from all over the world to pool their 'resources' 24 hours a day, 7 days a week. Chat features even allow users to interact as they share files.

Security risks
There is a very real security risk to every user who chooses to use P2P file-sharing software.

P2P software leaves your computer open to other users, and the files you download could be infected with trojans, worms or viruses – potentially leaving your computer vulnerable to attack or misuse. Keep in mind, too, that the filesharing software itself could install malware or spyware on your computer.

Legal implications
Individuals who share personal copies of film, television or music files on the Internet are at risk for lawsuits. We are sure you've seen many stories on this topic in the news over the past several years.

■ The above information is from the CyberAngels website which can be found at www.cyberangels.org, or see page 41 for address details.

© CyberAngels

■ The Internet is made up of millions of computers linked together around the world in such a way that information can be sent from any computer to any other 24 hours a day. (page 1)

■ The Internet is often described as 'a network of networks' because all the smaller networks of organisations are linked together into the one giant network called the Internet. All computers are pretty much equal once connected to the Internet, the only difference will be the speed of the connection which is dependent on your Internet Service Provider and your own modem. (page 1)

■ Three-quarters (75%) of 9- to 19-year-olds have accessed the Internet from a computer at home. (page 3)

■ Children usually consider themselves more expert in using the Internet than their parents – 28% of parents who use the Internet describe themselves as beginners compared with only 7% of children who go online daily or weekly. (page 4)

■ The number of e-shoppers now stands at 16 million. (page 5)

■ About 4.2 million people now spend £600 or more online every six months. (page 7)

■ 68% of men and 62% of women had used the Internet ever in 2005. (page 8)

■ More than seven in ten people (77%) say they will do their banking and pay their bills (72%) online in the next five years. (page 12)

■ There is evidence in the UK of a digital divide with some groups largely excluded from benefiting from access to the Internet for a variety of reasons including cost, lack of confidence or skills in using computers, and relevance. (page 13)

■ 36 per cent of people surveyed from the UK, Germany and the US said they spent an hour or more a day at work writing or reading personal emails – although the figure for the UK alone was lower at 27 per cent. (page 15)

■ The global nature of the Internet means it is very difficult to formally regulate it in the same way as other means of mass communication such as television, radio or offline publications. There is no central international body that monitors or approves Internet content before it appears online. (page 18)

■ As many as one in eight parents (13 per cent) do not know if their child uses chat rooms. (page 20)

■ 73 per cent of network managers would not report illegal images of children to the police, despite internally disciplining the employee committing the offence. (page 24)

■ 89% of British adults agreed that there should be a great deal or fair amount of co-operation between the UK police and international law enforcement agencies to help improve child safety online. (page 25)

■ The Internet is facilitating a major increase in children and young people being exposed to a wide range of age-inappropriate or illegal sexual and other kinds of material. (page 26)

■ 55% of illegal online content comes from the USA. Only 1% can be traced to the UK. (page 28)

■ The number of people cautioned or charged with child pornography offences in 2003 was 2,234, up from only 549 in 2001. This is also a huge increase of 6,500 per cent since 1988 – when the current legal framework for child pornography offences was established and only 35 cases were recorded. (page 29)

■ Spam is junk or unsolicited email. Often, spam is used to advertise (or spamvertise) services or goods of dubious, or even illegal, nature. (page 30)

■ Phishing is the name given to the practice of sending emails at random purporting to come from a genuine company operating on the Internet, in an attempt to trick customers of that company into disclosing information at a bogus website operated by fraudsters. (page 32)

■ In the early 90s, psychiatrists and clinicians were beginning to hear of a new medical term, 'Internet addiction'. At first, this was met with a lot of scepticism and denial, however, it became evident that the more people logged on to cyberspace, the more they got hooked. (page 36)

■ The average cost of making, marketing and distributing a movie is about $143m, and the average number of movies swapped on peer-to-peer networks in the United States each day is between 115,000 and 148,000. (page 38)

■ File-sharing networks have become wildly popular, they allow individuals to download games, applications, music and movies and more virtually for free. They are simple to use, and allow people from all over the world to pool their 'resources' 24 hours a day, 7 days a week. (page 39)

ADDITIONAL RESOURCES

You might like to contact the following organisations for further information. Due to the increasing cost of postage, many organisations cannot respond to enquiries unless they receive a stamped, addressed envelope.

British Market Research Bureau (BMRB)
Hadley House
26-30 Uxbridge Road
Ealing
LONDON
W5 2BP
Tel: 020 8433 4000
Fax: 020 8433 4001
Email: web@bmrb.co.uk
Website: www.bmrb.co.uk

Childnet International
Studio 14
Brockley Cross Business Centre
96 Endwell Road
LONDON
SE4 2PD
Tel: 020 7639 6967
Fax: 020 7639 7027
Email: info@childnet-int.org
Website: www.childnet-int.org
Childnet International was established as a non-profit organisation in 1995 with the mission to help make the Internet a great and safe place for children and to ensure that their interests are promoted and protected.

CyberAngels
Guardian Angels
Cyberangels Program
P O Box 3171
Allentown, PA 18106
USA
Tel: +1 610 377 2966
Fax: +1 640 377 3381
Email: webmaster@cyberangels.org
Website: www.cyberangels.org
Cyberangels is the largest online safety, education and help group in the world. They are a cyber-neighbourhood watch and they operate worldwide in cyberspace through more than 3,000 volunteers from more than fourteen countries.

GetNetWise
Internet Education Foundation
1634 1st Street, NW Suite 1107
Washington DC 20006
USA
Tel: 001 206 638 4370

Fax: 001 202 637 0968
Website: www.getnetwise.org
GetNetWise is a public service brought to you by Internet industry corporations and public interest organisations to help ensure that families have safe, constructive, and educational or entertaining online experiences. The GetNetWise coalition wants Internet users to be just 'one click away' from the resources they need to make informed decisions about their family's use of the Internet.

Internet Services Providers' Association UK
The Workshop
46B Tottenham Lane
LONDON
N8 7ED
Tel: 0870 0500 710
Email: admin@ispa.org.uk
Website: www.ispa.org.uk
The Internet Services Providers' Association (ISPA UK) is the UK's Trade Association for providers of Internet services. Visit their website for more information or contact them at the address above.

Internet Watch Foundation (IWF)
5 Coles Lane
OAKINGTON
Cambridge
CB4 5BA
Tel: 01223 237700
Fax: 01223 235870
Email: admin@iwf.org.uk
Website: www.iwf.org.uk
The Internet Watch Foundation (IWF) was launched in late September 1996 by Pipex to address the problem of illegal material on the Internet, with particular reference to child pornography. It is an independent organisation to implement the proposals jointly agreed by the government, the police and the two major UK service provider trade associations, ISPA and LINX.

Milly's Fund
PO Box 470
Case House
WALTON ON THAMES
Surrey
KT12 3XZ
Tel: 01932 235999
Email:
millysfund@elmbridgehousing.org.uk
Website: www.millysfund.org.uk
The charity aims to promote public safety, and in particular the safety of children and young people with the provision of training and education to teachers, youth workers, children and young people.

MORI (Market & Opinion Research International Limited)
79-81 Borough Road
LONDON
SE1 1FY
Tel: 0207 347 3000
Fax: 0207 347 3800
Website: www.mori.com

NCH
85 Highbury Park
LONDON
N5 1UD
Tel: 020 7704 7000
Fax: 020 7226 2537
Website: www.nch.org.uk
NCH improves the lives of Britain's most vulnerable children and young people by providing a diverse and innovative range of services for them and their families and campaigning on their behalf.

Pipex Communications
Carlton House
27A Carlton Drive
LONDON
SW15 2BS
Tel: 0870 909 8000
Email: contactus@pipex.net
Website: www.pipex.net
As the UK's first commercial ISP, Pipex has been a market leader for over a decade. They were the first ISP to bring the Internet to UK businesses.

INDEX

ACKNOWLEDGEMENTS

The publisher is grateful for permission to reproduce the following material.

While every care has been taken to trace and acknowledge copyright, the publisher tenders its apology for any accidental infringement or where copyright has proved untraceable. The publisher would be pleased to come to a suitable arrangement in any such case with the rightful owner.

Chapter One: Our Internet Society

An introduction to the Internet, © State of Victoria (Department of Education and Training), Initiative of DE&T, UK children go online, © London Schoool of Economics, E-shopping continues to surge, © British Market Research Bureau (BMRB), Internet shopping © CyberAngels, They flash their cash with a click, © BMRB, The guide to online grocery shoppers, © BMRB, Transforming learning and children's services, © Crown copyright is reproduced with permission of Her Majesty's Stationery Office, Old-fashioned education?, © Telegraph Group Limited, London 2005, Internet to change the face of banking in five years, © Pipex, The digital divide, © Crown copyright is reproduced with permission of Her Majesty's Stationery Office, Ten years of Cyberia, © Telegraph Group Limited, London 2005, Email to all staff . . ., © 2005 Associated Newspapers Ltd, Trust in online resources, © MORI, Information wants to be liquid, © Wired.

Chapter Two: Dangers of the Internet

Opportunites and risks go hand in hand, © IWF, The Internet, © IWF, The Internet – it's a real world out there!, © Childnet, Parents must act on online safety advice, © ISPA, Internet safety by age, © Get Netwise, Illegal images of children go unreported, © IWF, The Virtual Global Taskforce, © IWF, Child abuse, child pornography and the Internet, © NCH, Personal safety tips, © Milly's Fund, New centre to protect children online, © Crown copyright is reproduced with permission of Her Majesty's Stationery Office, Internet pornography offences quadrupled in two years, © NCH, Spam, © CyberAngels, Phishing, © BankSafeOnline, Pharming out-scams phishing, © Wired, Chat and instant messaging, © CyberAngels, Dealing with computer and Internet addiction, © AskMen, Hollywood heads to court over movie-swapping, © 2005 CNET Networks, Inc. All Rights Reserved, File sharing, © CyberAngels.

Photographs and illustrations:

Pages 1, 14, 17, 32, 38: Simon Kneebone; Pages 4, 26, 35: Bev Aisbett; Pages 6, 21: Pumpkin House; Pages 8, 24, 34: Don Hatcher; Pages 9, 30: Angelo Madrid.

Craig Donnellan
Cambridge
September, 2005